Praise for Mixed

"Since I've known him, I have seen Eli lead the next generation in a powerful way. In an age where identity politics and social disruption are raising new questions and demanding answers from the church, Eli, from his personal experience, provides a powerful kingdom way forward. Through *Mixed*, he offers a vulnerable window into the importance of finding one's God-led identity. Eli's story and in-depth look at Jesus invite us into this timely and complex conversion around what it means to be human."

—Dr. Rob Hoskins, President of OneHope

"It is one thing to pray for an answer; it is another to receive an answer. But it is best to BE an answer. Eli's book *Mixed* is an answer—a well prepared, biblically solid response to the conundrum of identity in our culture!"

—Bishop Dale C. Bronner, Founder and Senior Pastor
of Word of Faith Family Worship Cathedral

"*Mixed* both challenged and comforted me by revealing that Christ had an accent and a mixed background. Maybe I had chosen not to see it when reading the Word, as I have chosen to ignore some of my shortcomings in handling the tensions of living in a mixed society. I might have lost patience with Christ if I needed help with directions to Nazareth. Eli helped me realize I was too busy hiding my struggle and pain of being a Mexican American, Christian woman that is nei-ther here nor there in almost every circle I walk in. *Mixed* comforted me by reminding me of my identity in that mixed Savior."

—Rosie Rivera, Speaker and Author of *God*
Is Your Defender and *My Broken Pieces*

"Our world is growing increasingly complex, and there's absolutely no sign of that slowing down. This is especially true in the area of identity and figuring out how we belong in a multiethnic culture and society where we find more and more individuals who themselves are mixed in ethnicity. This hits home personally for me as my children are half Indian and half white, or as they refer to themselves—mixed. Eli reminds us we aren't in need of a new or novel approach to see the intrinsic value and worth of people. Rather, we need to reexplore the story of Jesus and see how his own upbringing (sadly often overlooked) gives us intimate insight into the importance of all people, and especially those of us that are mixed or raising mixed children in a highly diverse world. Eli is practical, vulnerable, winsome, and most important, theological in his approach in *Mixed*."

—JOEL MUDDAMALLE, PhD, DIRECTOR OF THEOLOGY
AND RESEARCH AT PROVERBS 31 MINISTRIES

"When I first heard Eli speak, I immediately thought, he should write a book on that! This is why I'm so excited that he did! *Mixed* will take you on a complex journey that will be both uncomfortable and encouraging, disruptive and comforting. While navigating delicate topics like multiethnicity in America, the politics of race, and divisions in the church over cultural topics, Eli keeps the gospel at the forefront of everything he says. Eli's brutal honesty combined with Christ-like humility made this book very hard to put down."

—PRESTON SPRINKLE, PhD, BESTSELLING
AUTHOR, INTERNATIONAL SPEAKER, AND HOST
OF *THEOLOGY IN THE RAW* PODCAST

"Eli has a unique wisdom and understanding of culture, the church, and the current generation. In *Mixed*, he brings much needed clarity around identity, purpose, and the way we see the world. Allow him to be your guide for navigating the complex issues we are all facing today in leading well."

—BRAD LOMENICK, FOUNDER OF BLINC AND AUTHOR
OF H3 LEADERSHIP AND THE CATALYST LEADER

"Eli Bonilla is an important voice for the church to hear. His perspective represents a new generation hungry to wrestle with the complexities of faith applied in our complex cultural moment. *Mixed* offers a window into the conversations Christians must have. It's an invitation to know God better by understanding one another more."

—GABE LYONS, FOUNDER OF Q IDEAS, COAUTHOR OF *GOOD FAITH* AND *THE NEXT CHRISTIANS*, AND COHOST OF *RHYTHMS FOR LIFE* PODCAST

"I have personally benefited from conversations with Eli on complex issues such as race and faith. He is wise beyond his years, and he leaves room for discussion and disagreement. In the pages ahead, as we realize we are all mixed, Eli reminds us where our identity comes from and why that matters most."

—JONATHAN POKLUDA, LEAD PASTOR OF HARRIS CREEK BAPTIST CHURCH, BESTSELLING AUTHOR, AND HOST OF *BECOMING SOMETHING* PODCAST

"The church is not made of a single color, race, language, or cultural context, but of all those who have accepted Jesus as Lord and have chosen to be His disciples. As interracial marriages become increasingly common, *Mixed* is a timely guide for helping this and future generations, including my own Guatemalan American children, not feel left out or out of place, but instead find their identity in Christ. It is the beauty and strength of the church to be mixed. It is our superpower."

—ANGEL JORDAN, DIRECTOR OF HISPANIC INITIATIVES FOR BILLY GRAHAM EVANGELISTIC ASSOCIATION

"Diversity isn't a current hot topic in the church. It's the future reality of the church. Minorities will soon be the majority in our nation and whatever church takes that conversation seriously today will be the church to reach the generation tomorrow. Eli Bonilla is one of the best communicators I've ever heard on the topic. *Mixed* will give you a peek into one of the most important conversations and shockingly underrepresented perspectives on the nuance of race."

—GRANT SKELDON, NEXT GEN DIRECTOR OF Q IDEAS AND AUTHOR OF *THE PASSION GENERATION*

MIXED

Embracing Complexity by Uncovering
Your God-Led Identity

BY ELI BONILLA JR.

W Publishing Group

An Imprint of Thomas Nelson

Mixed

Published in Nashville, Tennessee, by W Publishing, an imprint of Thomas Nelson.

Thomas Nelson titles may be purchased in bulk for educational, business, fundraising, or sales promotional use. For information, please email SpecialMarkets@ThomasNelson.com.

Any internet addresses, phone numbers, or company or product information printed in this book are offered as a resource and are not intended in any way to be or to imply an endorsement by Thomas Nelson, nor does Thomas Nelson vouch for the existence, content, or services of these sites, phone numbers, companies, or products beyond the life of this book.

ISBN 978-0-7852-9397-2 (audiobook)
ISBN 978-0-7852-9396-5 (eBook)
ISBN 978-0-7852-9349-1 (softcover)

Library of Congress Control Number: 2022947686

Printed in the United States of America
23 24 25 26 27 LBC 5 4 3 2 1

To my children, Ezekiel and Novalee,
may your identity always be found in Christ alone.

CONTENTS

CONTENTS

FOREWORD

Eli Bonilla Jr. is both deeply spiritual and cerebral. He has become an influential voice in our nation's cultural conversation regarding racial, ethnic, and spiritual identity.

Our society exhausts itself with conversations about differences based on one's nationality, ethnicity, race, or culture, not to mention education, occupation, and political preferences. Into this mess enters a Christian Hispanic Black man who has faced bigotry aimed at every one of those characteristics.

In this book, Eli challenges society's presuppositions and prejudices. He challenges us to think about how we relate to ourselves, as well as to God and others. He tackles the basic issue of all humanity—identity. Who are we? Where do we belong?

Today, people can sign up for "identity protection," which shields them from financial disaster. But people experience identity fraud with far more profound repercussions.

Scripture states that we have an enemy who comes to steal, kill, and destroy. Today, a very real enemy has created chaotic ideas and false precedents that fuel internal struggles.

Depression and suicide continue to spike as we grapple with our parentage, ethnicity, sexuality, and even the color of our own skin.

The resulting discontent within ourselves as individuals leads to discord in all our relationships. No wonder people struggle to accept others and build meaningful relationships. We don't even have a good relationship with ourselves. Without a clear understanding of our own identity, we will always have difficulty accepting ourselves and relating to others.

Often "I am" statements end negatively. People call themselves "losers," "victims," or "entitled." This type of self-talk is self-defeating. But, when the enemy comes to steal, kill, and destroy with such statements, Jesus gives us abundant life with a different kind of "I am" statement.

Moses was born a Hebrew slave, raised in Egyptian royalty, returned to his Hebrew roots, and ended up tending flocks as a foreigner in a wilderness far from the palaces or slave dwellings where he was raised. Amid his identity crisis, Moses had an encounter with God and asked Him who He was. God simply answered, "I am that I am." At that moment, Moses found his identity as God's child and recognized God's purpose and destiny for him.

Our "I am" statement can activate heaven and disengage hell for each of us. "I am" affirms our existence and validates our lives. It all begins not with "I was," "my parents were," or "I will be." Our personal "I am" begins with an encounter with our Creator. When we approach God through Jesus Christ, we can confidently say, "I am a child of God." We can say with absolute assurance, "I am uniquely created by God for a purpose and destiny," and "I am called and chosen."

When we meet God in his "I am," we discover our own "I am" because our truest identity statement begins with whom God says I am. We are not defined by what surrounds us but by God's Spirit that lives within us. We are not defined by past failures, generational curses, or current trends and prejudices. We are defined by God's love and eternal forgiveness. We are who God says we are.

When rejection and discouragement attempt to define us, we don't have to tolerate it. We can rise above perpetual victimization or entitlement and shout, "That's not who I am." With God's blessing, we push back against everything that raises its head against the knowledge of God in our hearts. We push back against an enemy that confines our identity to skin color, health, wealth, and pedigree by embracing the identity God gives us through his Word.

Having a strong grasp of personal identity derived from the Creator God is what led the ancients to act as they did, to face down pharaohs and lions, endure fiery furnaces, overcome violent persecution, and stand up for God against His enemies and theirs. It's what led them to write things like, "even in prison yet will I praise you" because they couldn't go anywhere, do anything, or face anything that threatened whom they knew themselves to be. That kind of perseverance derives from a foundation of identity.

My brother Eli is raising children with Dominican, Mexican, Anglo, and Palestinian heritages. Culture may try to place them in oversimplified boxes, categorizing them based on their differences and regarding them with prejudice or bigotry. In this book, aptly titled Mixed, Eli has provided his children and their future children a pathway to settle any identity crisis that may arise. It will do the same for you and your children and the next generation.

I encourage you to face today's complicated issues with courage, stop evaluating yourself by external means, and embrace the complexities of your existence so you can discover the blessing of being created as a unique being. Let Eli's words and tools, with their scriptural underpinnings, lead you to a greater reverence for God's divine design and a deeper relationship with him that leads you to a louder "I am," a stronger identity, and a more abundant life.

—REV. SAMUEL RODRIGUEZ
LEAD PASTOR OF NEW SEASON CHURCH, PRESIDENT
AND CEO OF NATIONAL HISPANIC CHRISTIAN
LEADERSHIP CONFERENCE, AUTHOR OF *PERSEVERE WITH POWER*, AND EXECUTIVE PRODUCER OF *BREAKTHROUGH* AND *FLAMIN' HOT*

INTRODUCTION

Hi. I'm Eli, and I'm mixed.

Now, when I say that, and you've seen my picture on the back cover, you probably have an idea of what that means. Maybe you could make that statement with your name too. Or maybe that's not how you would describe yourself. But I know you have an identity—and sometimes it bumps against the labels culture tries to put on you, just like mine does. How do I know this? Because defying labels is a human thing, and it seems to be front and center in so many conversations these days. That's why this book exists.

Mixed was written through the lens of a multiethnic millennial (me) trying to make sense of the conversations the world is having about identity. When group dynamics hinge on shallow concepts like physical appearances and stereotypical cultural distinctions, what happens to those of us who don't quite fit the mold of any particular group? We are all much more complex than our labels might suggest.

As I've tried to determine where and how I belong in this world, I've asked a lot of questions. What if the conversations we've had around identity, inclusion, and unity have been built on a faulty foundation? What if, at best, these conversations address superficial similarities between people but leave out those who have grown up in the borderlands of culture? What about those of us who are the by-products of a mixed-race or mixed-ethnic relationship? Or those of us who simply feel like we don't fit in, for whatever reason?

Where can we begin to build a healthier understanding of ourselves?

In turn, how can we love, celebrate, and unite people who are not simply different from one another but beautifully complex in their own ways?

Being mixed is the racial and ethnic reality of my life. Truly, this book was birthed from a life of tension, ambiguity, and having no clear-cut answers. This is the nature of the beast. I've experienced life in a culture that claims to be inclusive and to allow people to be free in their identities, but that couldn't be further from the truth. It turns out that what I've been searching for has less to do with *where I fit in* and more to do with *who I am*.

But this isn't just about me. It's about the future. This book is also an attempt to leave a tangible anchor for my children, who are currently one and three years old, as they navigate their even more mixed reality than mine. With Dominican, Mexican, Palestinian, and American heritages rooted in their DNA, they will one day grapple with their identities and craft their worldviews, and I hope this book gives them, and other kids like them, support and wisdom. The more I think, research, and speak about being mixed, the more I realize that this topic goes well beyond the confines of those in the mixed race and ethnic community. There is a bigger story on identity that can include everyone.

In 2021 at a conference, I spoke about what I call "The Forgotten Minority." After giving my talk, I was sitting in the audience when I heard another speaker say, "If you don't understand the story you're living in, you can't understand the story you're living out." That line stuck with me. *What is the story we're living in?*

The words came from Thabiti Anyabwile, a pastor speaking to Christian leaders who were exploring controversial topics concerning the church and culture. "Pastor T," as he's known, was talking about the Black and white racial narrative of America, showing leaders that in order to have a more complete understanding of racism—what it is, when we first see it pop up in history and why—we need to look at it in the context of the Bible first, and then human history. Because when we all have a more nuanced understanding of the *who*, *what*, and *why* around racism, we're more able to move forward together as a people.

The book of Genesis tells us that we were beautifully created in the image of God, but we are corrupted by sin from the fall of humanity. History is filled with people building out of brokenness and then turning around to produce even *more* brokenness. Sometimes it feels like there's no end in sight for how much more fractured and complicated this cultural story built by humanity will become.

And so, as we explore what it means to be *mixed*, you and I are going to consider the story we've been living in.

My hope is to expose the faulty foundation of our cultural narrative and show how we are better off listening to God as he invites us to be a part of his greater story. We need to step out of the story we've written for ourselves and remember that we're part of a much larger and older story, one that stems from beyond time and into eternity. This story has a beginning and end that are already written. And the author is the one true God, the one who is our Creator and whose reputation is "Finisher."

Now, stepping into this larger story won't provide all the granular clarity we might like around the many dimensions that shape a God-led identity. After all, Jesus repeatedly entered into conversations that didn't have easy answers or traditional prescriptions. In many ways Jesus was more about questions than answers.

But as messy as it feels, I believe we can find peace in our complexity. This book will look at several components of finding that peace.

First, I'll share my own story as a young, mixed Latino tossed into the fires of controversy around the topic of race during a heated cultural moment. That's when I felt the need for a deeper understanding of why, how, and for what we were created.

My story is closely tied to issues of race, but this is not a book about race at its core. Rather, it's a book about God-led identity. No one fits into a box. No one person is an identical copy of anyone else. As life shapes us, it produces radiant distinctions between people. Regardless of our outer appearances, the mixture of life's experiences is unique to each person. That's why I'll invite you to consider various ways *you* are mixed. We'll highlight the social, cultural, experiential, and racial/ethnic components of identity and how they all can be reconciled for God's purpose for our shared *imago Dei*. The goal is to see how God weaves our lives' stories together as a tapestry, one that shows our unique places in the body of Christ and our unique assignments on earth.

Next, we will dive into the complexity of Jesus' own journey of identity and cultural pressures while on earth. Whether it was the devil tempting him in Matthew 4 (with statements like, "If you are the Son of God . . ."), the pressure from his disciples to be an earthly king who would topple the Roman Empire, or the moments when the tensions of his eternal assignment from his Father conflicted with his earthly relationships with his mother and siblings, Jesus repeatedly defied expectations.

The way he navigated these situations is a model of how we as believers can live in a world that seems hostile to Christianity but still maintain our convictions and identities in Christ.

Finally, we'll explore what it looks like to embrace a mixed identity and live on a mission—a mission from God. Paul did it. A lot of our Bible heroes did it, as human and complex as they were. And because God calls us to live out a calling, he equips us as well. With everything we are and everything we're not, all of this works together to equip us in unique ways for our unique assignments.

Again, I use the term *mixed* not only for racial or ethnic categorization but also for the complexity of the human experience. You don't need to have a mixed heritage to gain a deeper sense of God's design and purpose for your life. *Mixed* is for everyone who has felt left out and out of place. This can happen among people who look like you, people from the same place as you, and even immediate family. Who hasn't experienced that kind of disconnect at one point or another?

But let's discover the blessing in not being like anyone else. When you embrace your complexity, you can start to see God's ability to use even the most obscure parts of your story for his divine purposes—how every aspect can be utilized to bless those around you. It's not about the exclusion of anything but about the alignment of everything. God can use it all so you can become a conduit of hope into a broken world.

Honestly, my goal with this book is not to provide clear-cut answers as to why you were born with the set of variables you've had to grapple with. You probably won't walk away believing you have it all figured out. But I do hope you will be equipped with the scriptures that point you to Jesus and the ways he showed us how to be human. I hope you'll also have more reverence for your divine design and a curiosity that will draw you closer and deeper into a relationship with your heavenly Father.

As you read, think of this discussion of the *mixed* life like a journey up a mountain. This mountain being one of tension, confusion, and uncertainty. I'm your humble Sherpa, and I invite you to climb with me to the peak, where you'll take in the view of where you've been and begin to form some level of clarity and meaning. As we climb the mountain, we'll make pit stops from camp to camp (aka chapter to chapter). Every chapter will give you a chance to rest and reflect, and perhaps think of how an issue applies to you. And along the way, I'll hand you tools to put in your bag—things I've learned from my own past climbs. Every story, thought, and example I'll share with you has helped me climb this mountain before.

You may not agree with everything in this book, and that's okay. Hang in there with me. At some level I want to challenge your presuppositions and make you think a little more deeply about how you relate to God, to others, and to yourself. If you're feeling these tensions, I have done my job.

So what does it mean to be *mixed*? Come with me. Let's get into this beautifully complex yet crucial conversation—together.

PART 1

MIXED UP

1

I'M CONFUSED

Can I Be Upset Too?

"I'm confused," said my Dominican mother in the summer of 2020.

Our family was participating in a public forum taking place in an African American church in the Eastside neighborhood of San Antonio, Texas, and my mother was puzzled by the conversation unfolding from city leaders, pastors, policemen, and local government officials. Most of the room was African American with several Anglo pastors and participants, and very few Latinos. My mother, father, and I were part of the small number of Latinos in the room; however, my mother and I were also a part of the larger populace of black constituents present. This duality came to a head in the mind of my mother in that moment. Having immigrated from the Dominican Republic to New Jersey, she already had a complicated past with African Americans, as many Afro-Latinos do in the Northeast United States. She would tell me stories of confrontations she had in her school and neighborhood growing up where the tension and division among Caribbean Afro-Latinos like Dominicans and African Americans spilled over into verbal and even physical bullying. Both black communities are very similar in appearance but divided by culture, language, and country of origin. So now that the conversation had landed on the racial category "Black," my mother felt the moment was right to bring clarity and depth to the conversation.

The country was fresh on the heels of the death of George Floyd. The tidal wave of civil unrest in our nation was being exacerbated by the growing undercurrent of past tragedies and broken systems. A pandemic had given us space to try to digest all that was going on. With the spotlight shining brighter than ever on the tensions between races in the United States, the faith community in San Antonio felt the need to act. So, to bridge racial relations and allow for raw and authentic conversations to take place, we found ourselves assembled in one room. My father, a Mexican immigrant and a prominent pastor of a large Spanish-speaking, immigrant church in our city, had brought my mother and me to the open forum.

Discussion reached a fever pitch, and the tension in the room was palpable. Then my mother walked up to the open microphone stationed in the middle of the room. With a look of exhaustion and pain, she uttered the words, "I'm confused." A hush came over the room. She continued, "I raised my son, a Black man, to live in a society that judges him by the color of his skin. We talked about issues related to race regularly. Yet I feel like today's conversation around race doesn't include us. We look the same as those fighting for their rights, but I've been told my whole life that I wasn't really 'Black' Black. So can I be angry? Can I be upset? I'm confused."

There was a pause, followed by an eruption of applause as the moderator said, "Yes, you indeed have the right to be upset too."

Like Mother, Like Son

For the first twenty or so years of my life, I checked the racial box marked "white" on education and governmental forms (per my teachers' guidance), but if you saw my mother, there would be no questioning her African ancestry. Whether it's the people living on the continent of Africa today, or the African Americans who spent centuries fighting for their rights, the blood in their veins runs in my mother's too. That blood is in me as well, and yet through years of being led to mark "white," I consistently chose to label myself that way.

It was not until my son, Ezekiel, was born at the beginning of 2021 that I made a different, and to some within the Dominican community, controversial choice. At the hospital, a nurse asked my wife and me to provide general information, including our racial identities, and after I paused a moment, I answered "Black."

My wife was pleasantly surprised, as she'd witnessed my identity crisis over the previous year. "Wow, babe, you've been talking about the opportunity to mark 'Black' as a Dominican for a while now," she said. "How does it feel?"

The nurse quickly interjected with a surprised yet kind response, saying, "Oh wow, I'm Dominican, and you're the first Dominican I've seen come through here who chose 'Black' as a racial distinction." (My wife later admitted that, at first, she had assumed our nurse was African American, but I, being Dominican, had realized she was Caribbean.)

I'm no hero for switching from "white" to "Black." I don't even believe in this system of racial categorization. But not shying away from what I knew to be true of my genetic makeup felt liberating even though I knew the system at play. For the first time ever, I embraced the African ancestry that, as my mother had taught me, made me different from others and informed my social interactions throughout my life.

Growing up in San Antonio provided the groundwork I needed to deal firsthand with these tensions I feel now. I was *ni de aquí, ni de allá,* a Spanish phrase used by second-generation Latinos meaning "not from here, or from there." It expresses the tension of being born to immigrant parents and raised in the United States. I had the added complication of not fitting into a predetermined racial category.

From the age of five until I graduated high school, I lived on the Northeast side of San Antonio. Our house was barely inside the affluent Northwood neighborhood—only two houses away from the edge of it. My father, who has been in full-time ministry my entire life, was able to move our family into the neighborhood through a personal connection. He was working at an Anglo-German church at the time, and an older white gentleman he knew from the church invited us to live in a house at the same price we were paying at an apartment complex. Neighborhood-wise, it was a huge leap for us.

It was a predominantly white neighborhood with only a few Hispanics—us and a Mexican immigrant family, who'd originally moved to Chicago, then relocated to San Antonio. (It was awesome to see the parties they threw, especially when they'd have a *banda*—a Mexican band—come and play concerts in their backyard during their *asada*—a Mexican cookout.) Apart from our family and theirs, the neighborhood had no real diversity. This sounds extreme, but truthfully, combined, we seemed to carry the diversity of our neighborhood on our backs. And this came with unforeseen rules of engagement.

As I grew up, I participated in school sports and wanted to go for runs in our neighborhood to build up my endurance. Every time I'd start getting dressed to go outside, though, my mother would catch me and ask me what I was planning to do. When I'd answer, she'd stop me in my tracks and sit with me on the couch. She did this a number of times, and the conversation always began with a lecture about where we lived and what I looked like. Essentially she was telling me that as a young Black man, I could not run in a white neighborhood because I might be mistaken for someone who was "up to no good."

Though I had never experienced anything like that in our neighborhood, my mother had grown up in New Jersey in the seventies and eighties and had plenty of stories to tell. Some involved difficult moments when the broader population identified her and her siblings by their skin color, not by their culture (though having an "immigrant family" status wouldn't have made things any better).

I was not about to argue with a Caribbean mother from the Northeast, so I let it go and took her word for it. I stayed home every time.

Then, years later, what I had thought to be improbable happened the day before my birthday in the winter of 2020. Ahmaud Marquez Arbery, a young Black man twenty-five years of age, was jogging in a residential neighborhood near Brunswick, Georgia, when he was pursued by three white men and gunned down on camera. The murder sent shockwaves through the country.

I had received an alert on my phone and seen the social media posts about the incident, but before I could respond to what was happening, I received a message from my mother: *Remember when we used to have our conversations about this?* Yes, I remembered. It made the news of the killing hit home.

Whether or not you can relate to this, please understand something: for a mother to have to sit her son down and explain he can't do something as innocent as jogging in an affluent neighborhood, or how critical it is that he obey traffic laws to avoid interactions with police, is heartbreaking. This sense of danger has been my reality my whole life, and when Ahmaud was killed, it became terribly amplified.

At the time, my wife and I lived in a diverse neighborhood on the Eastside of San Antonio, and, as many others did several days after the murder, we chose to run the neighborhood for 2.23 miles to remember the date this tragedy took place. I kept trying to process this chilling reality: *That could have been me.* I thought back to situations where I'd unknowingly been in danger because of the way I looked, where things could have played out differently.

Now, here is the curveball that hit me a few months later at the public forum. If my mother was confused about where she stood in her identity in this conversation, then where did *I* find myself? I was the son of a Mexican immigrant and a Dominican immigrant. I was born in California and raised in Texas. I pursued education in Louisiana, Oklahoma, and Tennessee. I wasn't African American or as dark-skinned as many Afro-Latinos were, but I was nowhere near being white as my government documents would suggest. I was as brown as they came, with African-leaning features and fine hair, which made for such a mixed bag of physical attributes that, at a glance, I could blend in almost anywhere among the majority world population. This made me feel like the whole world had room for me, but my own country didn't know what to do with me.

After the killing, I finally had a moment when I could truly identify with the conversation around Ahmaud. But the problem was, given my cultural makeup and mixed bag of features, I didn't fit the exact mold of the African American community, who were rightfully furious and publicly engaged in this fight for justice.

So, at that forum, I carried the same confusion as my mother—and then some.

If my mother was confused, then I was lost.

From Black and White to Technicolor

As the conversation around race moved at breakneck speed during the summer of 2020, I reached a pivotal moment—an existential crisis, really. All I'd felt, through a lifetime of struggling with my identity as a mixed kid, rose to the surface. The more I unpacked, the more I got the sense that I only superficially fit the mold of the conversation. Heck, I even found myself fitting in several molds of the conversation simultaneously.

My wife and I felt the brunt of this during a confrontation with a Black couple on a plane, with a young Black woman at the center of it. Before I dive into details, I want to be clear: As the son of a Black woman, with relatives and friends who are Black women, this in no way is a story supporting the evil and toxic view society has put on our Black women. It's a story about snapping tensions and the polarizing times we find ourselves in.

In the fall of 2020, several months after the open forum, my wife and I were traveling back and forth between Texas and Florida, looking for a new home in the Sunshine State. When our plane reached the gate at the Fort Lauderdale airport, my seven-months-pregnant wife gathered her things and made her way into the narrow plane aisle. Suddenly, she found herself in a tangle with an impatient young Black woman, who attempted to push her out of the way in the already too-small aisle. Moments later in the Jetway, as she and her husband passed us, the woman said, "See? Their people always trying to take everything from us!"—alluding to my wife and I taking up what she felt was more than our share of space in the plane aisle.

My wife is Palestinian American, the daughter of a Palestinian immigrant father and an Anglo-American mother, and she was wearing a mask due to COVID protocol. My wife did not shy away from exchanging words as the young lady continued to speak about the "privilege" that my wife and "her people" demonstrate daily.

Perhaps if my wife had not been wearing a mask, her features would've signaled that she was a part of the minority community, and the situation would not have escalated. But I honestly don't know if that would've been the case.

At this point I was boiling. In defense of my wife and in

an effort to defuse this conversation, I blurted out, "Hey! She's Palestinian American, and she's pregnant with my baby, who happens to be Black because he's Dominican, like me."

Immediately the woman turned around and said loudly, "Yeah? Well, I'm *real* Black!" She then started chanting loudly the acronym of the largest social justice movement at the time as we entered a crowded terminal.

I was so baffled it drew me to immediate silence. I had attended a couple of marches and had only recently felt free to accept my place within the diverse Black community. But suppressed memories from my childhood flooded back to me. Every time I tried my best to identify with either side of my heritage, I was accepted only to a certain extent. Every time I took a real swing at melding into the group as an equal, I would be met with a "Yeah, you're like us, but not really." I was Mexican, *but* I was Dominican. I was American, *but* I was . . . It went on and on.

I was "white" . . . well, who was I kidding? That was only for the sake of state-sanctioned tests and my driver's license. Now, I was Black *but*. The more I wandered into any given tribe and tried to fit in, the more my differences with it were illuminated.

I was realizing the inadequacy of the "Black" and "white" boxes I had been forced into. That "either/or" type of categorization doesn't allow for people to be more. I was caught in the in-between, hoping for a more vibrant world than the one that had been offered to me. It's like I wanted to go from black-and-white television to technicolor. I hoped and prayed that I wouldn't get stuck in the past of a washed-out and simplified conversation but instead be welcomed into a world that was compatible with the complexity of a vibrant conversation about the beauty of our humanity.

Living in the Hyphen

As a person of mixed race and ethnicity, I've often found myself navigating what Dr. Daniel Rodriguez, a professor of religion and Hispanic studies at Pepperdine University, calls "living in the hyphen," where I attempt to choose the best of multiple worlds.[1] Worlds that overlap. Like Texan-Californian-Afro-Latino-American. For those of us in the center of these overlaps, this mixture of appearance, culture, and accent leads to people misidentifying us, because they assume, perhaps based on their own experiences, we should be one thing and cannot be many things all at once.

If you can technically identify with multiple groups, how do you choose your identity (or can you even choose it)? Maybe a better question is: How do you choose which parts of your identity to embrace or express at any given time? For years I hid in my ambiguity, leaning into one part of my ethnic makeup while suppressing the others, then switching it up and emphasizing a different aspect of my identity. I would change accents when I could and dress differently when it served me better. If I were to choose my hierarchy of group identity, I would claim that it would go: (1) Texan, (2) Latino, and (3) American. (If you know Texans, then you know that for us this is an easy number one. There may not exist a greater pride in the world than the pride Texans have for Texas and being Texans.)

But it was hard to choose—especially when even the government couldn't decide how to label me. As I've mentioned, during the first two decades of my life I followed teachers' instructions to circle "white" rather than "Black" on racial categories, as was the custom of many institutions in the early 2000s. *Latino* was "white," because Latino was not a race. This is technically correct, in the sense that *Latino* is an ethnicity. But if you take a step back and look at the bigger picture, its narrow use is wrong. Latinos have representation across the spectrum of races. How this relates to selecting "white" or "Black" has long been a point of contention among the Latino community, but I was usually directed to circle "white," even with my dark-brown skin and distinct features.

If you find this as baffling as I did, hang tight for a minute. Let's further explore these definitions.

Which Is Which: Nationality, Ethnicity, Race, and Culture

Take another look at the title of this section. Do you know what those words *really* mean? If these terms make your head spin a little, you're not the only one. So let's take a minute to define the terms *nationality, ethnicity, race,* and *culture.*

A couple of years ago, I consulted with the Barna Group for their 2020 study called *Beyond Diversity: What the Future of Racial Justice Will Require of U.S. Churches.* I found their definitions for these four categorizations remarkably healthy, so we'll use them as a starting point:

> *Nationality* describes someone's legal status of citizenship or belonging to a particular nation.
>
> *Ethnicity* is based on perceived cultural similarities, which are often linked to a shared ancestral background or heritage. This may include someone's nationality, but ethnicity may also be defined by or exist in combination with their language, religion, tribe, or place of origin.
>
> *Race* is a set of socially created categories based on selected perceived differences in physical traits such as skin tone, facial features, hair texture, etc.
>
> *Culture* consists of beliefs, behaviors, objects, and other characteristics common to members of a particular group.[2]

Those definitions look pretty clear-cut on paper. But in life? Not so much. For children of immigrant parents, words like *nationality* and *culture* are tough realities to contend with. This is where terms like *third culture community* or *third culture kids* apply, where these individuals exist in an in-between space. They have to navigate a different culture at school or in the workplace after being raised in a home with a different dominant culture, the one of their immigrant parents.

Another way to talk about this tension is to use the example of Moses growing up in Egypt. Dr. Rodriguez says it this way:

Like many other native-born Latino Christians my spiritual pilgrimage resembled that of Moses. On the one hand, like Moses, I was raised and educated as an Egyptian (i.e., Anglo) in order to live and to succeed in Egypt (i.e., the United States). As a consequence of not speaking Spanish and not having an adequate appreciation . . . of my ancestral culture and homeland, I too was rejected by the Hebrews (i.e., foreign-born *mexicanos*) who contemptuously referred to me as . . . an anglicized Mexican.[3]

This references Dr. Rodriguez's upbringing as a second-generation Latino raised in the United States. Which is the same for me. For second-generation Latinos like me, adapting to the dominant culture often looks like not speaking Spanish fluently, if at all. It may also mean that we don't understand many cultural references—of either culture to which we belong. And like Moses, when we don't share these nuances with a particular culture, it might mean people in our own ethnicity reject us because we're "outsiders."

Ethnicity refers to shared cultural factors, including nationality, regional culture, ancestry, and language. It's estimated that there are currently 650 ethnic groups among the 190 recognized countries in the world.[4] When we're talking about different people groups in the Bible, using the word *ethnicity* is the most historically and contextually appropriate way to refer to someone's background, because it shows the layers of human complexities through the countless shifts in environment, culture, language, and more that each generation of characters had to go through.[5] In verses like Matthew 24:7 and Revelation 7:9, we see the Greek word *ethnos* is translated as "nation." And in places like Matthew 4:15 and Romans 11:13, the word *Gentile* refers to someone of non-Jewish descent. The Bible focuses on the shared identity of groups and links them together based on their mutual identity that goes far beyond where they live and what they look like.

Race historically has been used to define and categorize people by physical differences. For decades, censuses have used skin-deep metrics to blanket soul-deep complexity.

And *culture*? The definition of this concept is hazier than ever. In 2020, cultural confusion and uncertainty around national and global health policies, political leaders, and the definition of what was good and what was evil were already the theme of a COVID-filled year. But when all eyes were set on the growing racial tensions, more than ever I felt the pressure as a man of faith in the public eye to jump into helping however I could. Unfortunately, when you have to insert yourself into a conversation that may not have the room or bandwidth to talk about complexity, compromise is sure to creep in. I didn't perfectly fit in. I never had. Nothing made this more evident than that moment of conflict at the airport I'd have later that year.

My outsider status became obvious in less dramatic situations too: after awkward moments in conversations, when my gaps in cultural knowledge became clear, or when people ignored or dismissed me. When it came to group identity, I was always either missing something or held something that was given to me by others that I felt did not belong me.

With society's increasing tendency toward polarization and tribalism, a slight difference can become the weapon used to disqualify belonging. Physical and cultural differences stick out as irreconcilable and unchangeable obstacles to full acceptance from any of these groups, whether they're political, ethnic, generational, or otherwise. I could be a visitor to these groups that were a part of me, but I could never make my home with any of them. As I continued to unpack what I was feeling, I realized that this was not only limited to what I looked like but how I talked, what I believed, what I enjoyed, and where I grew up.

On top of this, I was also experiencing a crisis of faith after watching the responses of church culture on both sides of the conversation—and the lack of responses in other churches. With this came several primary questions:

Who is right?
Who is holding the real truth?
What is biblical justice?
How do we treat the image of God?
Where do I fit in this conversation?
How do I put my faith into action when the actions asked of me make me choose one part of my color or the other?
What am I?

To say I was having an existential crisis is an understatement. I felt like I was falling into an abyss of nothingness, trying to grasp some semblance of identity. The cultural conversations around "representation" or "inclusion" seemed to push me further into categories that I didn't completely fit into. It left me isolated in thought and exhausted in action.

I started posting on social media about my internal wrestling, and it resonated with many who had felt the same way or never considered this type of experience. Here is an excerpt of one of these posts:

> I fight for my beliefs, but am belittled by the side I fight for and the side I fight against. I'm not allowed to fully be upset or fully proud of any culture. I'm too Latino to be American, I'm too American to be Latino. I'm not African enough to have an opinion on BLM, I'm not Latino enough to have an opinion on the plight of the immigrant. . . . I'm too secular for Christians, but I'm too "church boy" for my lost friends. All the Mexicans who called me "Black Boy" growing up and all the Dominicans who called me "Beaner." All the times another Latino shamed me for not knowing enough Spanish and every American that commented on my accent or lack thereof.
>
> When you see me, who do you see?
> Where have you placed me?
> Am I like you? Am I like them?
> Can I be mad?
> Should I be content?
> Where do I lie according to your assumptions? . . .

Have you written me off?

Do you love me or my gift?

Do you want my view because you actually care or because you think it's the right thing to do?[6]

Many of those who read the post weren't racially mixed or on the fringes like I was, but they seemed to identify with it. We were in a tiring conversational structure of oversimplifying people and categorizing them by their differences.

The truth of the matter is, no one can be simply distilled into a category. At some point, given the right conversation, context, or cultural pressure, what you are mixed with will go to war within you.

Perhaps shortcomings in our conversations about things like race and ethnicity are just symptoms of a deeper confusion about identity. Perhaps our core struggle is understanding who we are as individuals, our relationships to or within the broader group, and what God could do with what he chose for us to be.

You see, I didn't choose to be mixed racially and ethnically. I didn't get to choose the parents I was born to or the state I was raised in. There are many things you didn't get to choose either. But the beauty of knowing why those elements of your life exist, both physically and experientially, will come from entering into the divine tension that comes with embracing who God created you to be. It will come when you wrestle through and learn to carry your identity well.

I'm mixed, and so are you.

Now let's dive in deeper and explore what that means for us.

2

SHOW ME YOUR ID

Identifiers Versus Identities

Middle school. **Perhaps the bumpiest time in any person's search for identity.** If I dug into old boxes and found my middle school ID card with a photo of little Eli on it, the picture would surely tell that story better than a thousand words. That's often the case with any old ID. You don't realize the transformative power of time until you've seen a picture of yourself from years ago. Whether that's looking thinner, darker, less wrinkly, or happier, every ID tells a story of becoming.

God has a better ID to reveal to us. This ID is the *imago Dei*, Latin for "image of God." This identity is about what is being redeemed in you. It holds a story that stems from the Creator himself. And my own journey toward discovering my

21

ID (*imago Dei*) was unknowingly sparked in my junior high years.

Like any middle school kid, I struggled to find myself. As I went from a fairly homogeneous environment of white kids in elementary school to a diverse middle school, I faced new peer pressure. Haircuts, fashion, and language became a big deal, playing a huge part in which group you wanted to accept you. I had to decide: Would I identify with kids from my old elementary school, or would I tap into my home and church culture and identify with the Latinos I was now surrounded by?

I chose Latino, and that meant I needed to change my look. My parents were pretty confused after I chose to lean into a more "urban" look, responding with, "Why did you cut your hair like that?" "Pull your pants up." "Wear normal socks" (back when no-show socks were in). My Puerto Rican uncle from the Bronx took me for my first "real" haircut at a barbershop. I wanted to look like my friends, who idolized Black culture, even though the majority were Latino and only a few were Black.

The side of town where I grew up was a mixed bag of communities. I mentioned that I technically lived in a mostly Anglo neighborhood, but it bordered housing projects toward the eastside of San Antonio, which at the time had a large African American population and a large Mexican population. This wasn't the case anywhere else in San Antonio. Having this mix of Mexicans and African Americans made for a lot of mistaken identity from my peers who couldn't quite put me in a box, but then I started wearing brands like Southpole, Rocawear, and Phat Farm (actually "Quicks" that were the flea market versions), along with baggier clothes, Jordans, tall tees, and oversized jerseys. I even picked up cussing to fit in, though I was pretty bad at it. I was desperate to be identified as someone worthy of acceptance, regardless of whether it flew in the face of what I was raised to believe.

My ID card in middle school reflected my physical appearance. Even today, I find that people study the way I look, searching for clues in my haircut, facial hair, and clothing to box me into a racial or ethnic category. Even after all that, I'm often misidentified.

I've had some pretty awkward encounters with officials who needed to see my ID card. One time a TSA officer looked at it and cleared me, and then moments later another TSA officer pulled me aside and asked for it again. He told me to cover my mouth to hide my beard, squinted at me, and said, "You must've gotten quite a tan," inferring I was much darker than my picture on my ID. I was indeed. The beard I was sporting was also new, and that darker skin and beard combo seemed to prompt the TSA officer to question some things about me. The picture was a couple of years old since I, like most people, avoid the DMV like the plague and had opted not to get a new picture for my ID, but I could see myself in that old picture just fine. The TSA official, not so much. This is only one of my many "random" security checks at an airport.

To be fair, any attempt to identify someone in a moment can result in an awkward situation like this. Such as having random languages spoken to you, which happens to me in major cities with diverse immigrant populations. Or when someone includes you in their racial ethnic group by saying, "They don't get us!" without even knowing you. Regardless, I have found myself in situations where I've been forced onto a side or with a group without even wanting to be there.

A Tale of Two Chicagos

One summer, I served at an urban outreach in Chicago with a group from my university. We spent our days serving at schools and at a church's vacation Bible school, and we spent our evenings experiencing the city. I'll never forget the first day debrief, when our intern director gave us precautions about visiting Humboldt Park, the area of town where we were staying. The neighborhood suffered from high crime rates and violence, so we were all ears to anything she could tell us about navigating our day to day. We had to walk everywhere or take public transit because none of us had cars (#internproblems).

Let me jump in and say that there were just five of us on this team. Four were female and white, so I truly was the odd man out. We were in a predominantly African American and Latino neighborhood segregated by various streets; depending on which street you turned down, you would see a different racial group. Being Afro-Latino, I felt like I could blend in pretty well and help the group navigate the waters of this cultural context.

I was thinking of this as our intern director was talking,

then I heard her direct a comment toward me. She began to give me a personalized warning about walking alone. Confused, I felt my emotions rise, protesting why I was the only one out of the five of us to be singled out. Not only could I blend in, but I also had years of inner-city ministry experience.

The intern director explained that it was rare to see white people in this neighborhood; here, white people were usually cops or lost tourists. This meant the girls had a built-in alibi. Then she turned to me. "You look too much like the people from here."

I quickly jumped to a "duh" in my mind—I knew the ethnic and racial makeup of the neighborhoods. But as I was mentally rebutting her, she went on to say that the gangs were very territorial. They were also broken up into various racial groups. Because I looked like I was from this area of Chicago and could pass for either African American or Latino, I could be mistaken for someone I wasn't. In that neighborhood, nothing would be more dangerous than being perceived as someone who couldn't be claimed by either side, making me a target of both sides. To my shock I found that, in this situation, my ability to be a chameleon was not an asset. More important than blending in is understanding who you are in relation to any given environment—and taking that on with a sense of respect and intentionality. That was especially important in this dangerous situation.

So, much to my embarrassment, she assigned me to always walk with the girls, just so I could be associated with their group, thus ensuring people would not categorize me as an unidentified local. I had expected to be the one protecting them, but ultimately, I was in need of the protection. Man, how the tables had turned.

Cultural confusion wasn't always life-or-death that summer. Chicago has a great "Little India," a portion of the city with many Indian and Pakistani shops and restaurants. I have always loved Indian food, so I suggested we go eat at one of the restaurants.

If there is any group of people outside of my actual ethnic group that I get confused with most often, it would be the Indian community. As a matter of fact, even Indian people have admitted to me they thought I was either Indian, Pakistani, Bengali, or Nepali.

I was the only person of color at our table at the Indian restaurant. I could see the waiter eyeballing me with the group of white young ladies, perhaps assuming I was their tour guide of Little India. At the end of the meal, he began speaking to me in his native dialect. Being bilingual, I am frequently the one interpreting Spanish for those who don't speak the language (and as Spanish is the second most-spoken language in the United States, I've had plenty of opportunities). But now I was lost. I was embarrassed not to pick up on any of the words or have someone from our group interpret. I guess embarrassment was mixed with a little social anxiety as well, because I took a shot at understanding him (which I would not advise in any cross-cultural situation). I treated his comment like a yes or no question, and I nodded my head yes. He nodded back, then quickly walked away and into the kitchen.

The next thing I knew he was heading back to our table with both the check and six boxes of rice in two large white bags. Once again, in my embarrassment and lack of willingness to correct or confront, I accepted the check and the boxes of rice. I can't be certain what he had said exactly, but whatever I'd agreed to left me with loads of rice to take back to intern housing—which, by the way, was on the other side of Chicago and could only be reached by a lengthy ride on public transportation. Try sitting on a bus in the middle of summer with what feels like thirty pounds of steaming rice wedged between you and a bunch of strangers for ninety minutes!

For you, this lesson is free. This lesson cost me money, energy, and comfort. Be humble and politely admit you can't understand someone—or roll the dice and spend too much money and energy pretending to be something you're not for the sake of a stranger. Honesty is the best policy, my friend.

Considering how I've encountered other people's wrong assumptions about me leads us to another question: How can we get past our assumptions about people based on their physical appearances? What questions should we ask? We can't always determine how we will be treated, whether in a life-and-death situation, like my time in Humboldt Park, or a simple misunderstanding in a restaurant. But we can try to find a common place to launch from that will help people feel seen in a deeper way than what appearances can reveal.

Better Questions

"What are you?"

Ah, that famous line uttered in the direction of a racially or ethnically ambiguous individual. Most of the time I can assume what they mean. At the core of the question could be a couple of things. On one end of the spectrum, it's pure curiosity. They're either assuming one thing and seeking confirmation (usually from one brown person to another), or they're just genuinely confused about identifying you as an individual. On the other end of the spectrum are those who desire to categorize you, making their interaction with you simple and digestible, or even weighing whether to write you off because of it.

I have gotten these questions more times than I can count. And because I've hit the brown-people jackpot of genetic features that could categorize me from Bengali to Brazilian, people seem to talk themselves in and out of a label until they give up and ask: "What are you?"

I must say, "What are you?" makes me feel more like an object than a human. "Who are you?" implies a different intent related to the essence of the person.

This perhaps should be a red flag to all of us. Why do we ask what we ask? Appearance isn't everything, but appearance does affect interactions throughout our lifetimes. Skin color, facial features, height, weight, gender—there is so much variation in appearance that drives and shapes our lives, it becomes impossible to avoid, and it should not be avoided. But the question "What are you?" emphasizes *what* you look like rather than *who* you are. I believe these two things are interwoven and can enrich each other when the *who* comes before the *what*.

Usually when someone asks me "What are you?" my answer is, "What do you mean?" Then the person will ask, "Where are you from?" This has been the question I have received both domestically and internationally, and my response never seems to satisfy.

"I was born in California and raised in Texas," I'll say. This will be met with a no—they will literally tell me, "No . . ." And I'm like, *Hold up, dude. I'm out here trying to be kind with my answer and you're telling me no?!* But the person always immediately follows up with, "Where are your parents from?" Then the conversation starts to hit a rhythm when I explain my Dominican and Mexican roots.

Many times I end up explaining a lot about myself, because in order to really know someone, you need to understand the context in which they were raised and formed. This plays a huge role in the way both people in the conversation see the world, and it also welcomes an outsider into *your* particular world, with all its nuance and complexity.

In my opinion a better question would be, "What is your heritage?" But I wouldn't make this my first question. "Tell me about yourself," might be better.

Curiosity is in our nature, and seeing someone who holds an obvious distinction can draw out that curiosity. A lot of times, it feels like starting a conversation about race and ethnicity (just because you want to scratch that curiosity itch!) leads to dead-end conversations. Once the itch is scratched, at best the fire for conversation dissipates. At worst, it can come across like you've tried to box someone into something they didn't choose to be. But if you approach the conversation asking about "who" a person is rather than "what" they are, your tone sounds more genuine and caring.

Our personal intentions should be linked to our *imago Dei*. We should see others as people made in the image of God and then fight to stay mindful of their humanity, not the categories we've been fed. So here's what I'd do: I'd start with, "Tell me about yourself," then move to, "Wow! I'd love to hear more about how you grew up." That kind of curiosity, one that puts the humanity of that person before anything else, can be a gateway into a deeper understanding. It makes the *what* questions (about their accent, style, and physical appearance) a by-product of a *who* conversation.

As we get to know one another in a real way, we move past our assumptions and gain an appetite for the complexity of people, rather than assuming simplicity. Regularly interacting with people on deeper levels can shape our mindsets of how we view everyone. After all, we know there's always more than meets the eye. Each person God created is beautifully complex and distinct.

I expect I'll have more encounters with people approaching me with a "What are you?" question. My response will probably start with, "It's not that simple."

It's Not That Simple

At the beginning of 2021, a prominent American megachurch invited several young Christian Latino leaders and me into a conversation about how churches could properly include Latinos in leadership and church culture. It was a weekend gathering that included attending a Sunday service, meeting with the church's amazing group of campus pastors, and each guest giving a presentation on the Christian Latino perspective. Each of my peers presented phenomenal thoughts around this subject, but one of the presentations hit me between the eyes.

My friend Emmanuel got up and presented a talk he called "It's Not That Simple." Mind you, there was a mixed bag of Latinos present—Caribbeans, South Americans, and North Americans. We had a lot of corners covered. Emmanuel, a Dominican American from Washington Heights, New York, had been in the majority population of his East Coast neighborhood, but now he was in the minority at a predominantly and historically white church in rural Texas. Through all this, he experienced a spectrum of awakening that he shared with the group that was similar to what I'd gone through.

One of the stories he shared was about a couple who had moved to the US from Australia to plant a church. Upon arriving in the United States, the wife took her four children to the doctor's office and asked how she should check a racial category on the medical form. Both she and her husband were aboriginal, members of the native people of Australia, and had never been confronted with the racial categorization of "Black" and "white" before. She was fair-skinned, and her husband was darker skinned, and the appearances of their four beautifully mixed children varied on a spectrum of color. The nurse quickly assessed the situation and reassured the mother that the question and boxes were very "simple." She pointed to the two children who were on the fairer side and said that they were "white" and that the darker-skinned children were to be considered "Black."

This was an unforeseen shift for the identity of this family, especially given the contextual and historical whiplash of the "Black and white" binary in America, which is not manifested the same way in Australia. For the sake of simplicity and "understanding," people would divide a family by these terms, even when they didn't really fit into those boxes.

This has also been the plight of Latino Americans who are a mixture of all races and not able to fit neatly into color categories. As my friend Emmanuel went on to say, "We like when things are simple. We like when things make sense to us. Because we want to live a life of understanding." My Pentecostal heart almost made me physically jump out of my seat to take a lap around our meeting room. That was exactly what I'd been wrestling with!

We all are longing for understanding, and that often leads us to oversimplify infinitely complex individuals created by a God who knit every piece of them together. The truth is, it's an act of faith to let another person guide you beyond the shallow end of their appearance and into who they are. This is what the basis of relationship is. We allow the other person to reveal who they are without knowing or understanding everything. We let others humbly remind us that we are more than our physical identifiers.

Now, I need to be clear: Our *identifiers*—how we look—do play a role in shaping our experiences in society. I'd never want to dismiss the beauty of our diverse appearances, and I'm not advocating for color blindness, which is an indictment of how wonderfully complex God has created humanity. I appreciate how pastor and author Dr. Derwin Gray uses the term "color blessed" instead of "color-blind."[1]

Let's see how we can go beyond *simple* and wade into the beautiful complexity that lies beneath the surface.

Don't Judge a Book by Its Cover

Have you ever used the phrase, "You can never judge a book by its cover"? For the most part, it's a lesson about prejudice of the eye. Rarely, if ever, are we open-minded enough to avoid letting any assumption, prejudice, projection, or jadedness inject itself into a moment of visual perception. According to a Princeton study, psychologists found that we make our initial judgments of a person in the first one-tenth of a second. Alexander Todorov, one of the psychologists in the study, stated,

We decide very quickly whether a person possesses many of the traits we feel are important, such as likeability and competence, even though we have not exchanged a single word with them. It appears we are hard-wired to draw these inferences in a fast, unreflective way.[2]

The researchers also found that the length of time subjects looked at someone's face after their initial judgments didn't sway their initial opinions. If anything, they became more confident in their judgments, almost as if convincing themselves of their own reliability.

We often walk away from interactions with others holding one of two thoughts: *They were exactly who I thought they were,* or *That went totally different than I expected.* This goes for both negative and positive experiences.

My hope is that we would continually grow in our openness to the unknown and move away from categorically typecasting people in an unhealthy way. You can't stop analyzing people at a glance, during a first interaction, or even after years of knowing someone. That's human. What you *can* attempt to do is to listen to that person with intention and interact with them. When you do that, you're one step closer to moving past what your eye test is asking you to accept. That, I think, is divine.

Fortunately for us, the Bible is filled with moments that teach us this. Moments when people were counted out because of their appearance but whom God used nonetheless. Perhaps one of the most famous examples is when the Lord asked the prophet Samuel to go to the house of Jesse and anoint the next king of Israel. Jesse had a large family with several sons, the youngest of whom was David, who (spoiler alert) was to become the greatest king in Israel's history. Here's what the book of 1 Samuel tells us:

> When they arrived, Samuel saw Eliab and thought, "Surely the LORD's anointed stands here before the LORD." But the LORD said to Samuel, "Do not consider his appearance or his height, for I have rejected him. The LORD does not look at the things people look at. People look at the outward appearance, but the LORD looks at the heart." (16:6–7)

Let me give a little bit of background (and offer a little sympathy in defense of Samuel and his quick judgment call).

Eliab was the oldest son, and in that time and culture—in Israel around 1000 BC—the eldest son was the father's heir apparent in resources and honor. Being the eldest afforded you privilege and prestige. So, especially given the limited information Samuel had, it wasn't crazy for him to assume that things had lined up for Eliab to receive the honor of kingship.

This passage also describes Samuel's reaction to physical appearance. Eliab had height and good looks. Was Samuel a fool? I don't believe so. If anything, Samuel was one of the greatest prophets of the Old Testament. But he had already encountered a man who fit this description before: Saul, the now-rejected king of Israel. Though appearance wasn't the reason he was selected, it would stand to reason that Saul, being the first and only king that Samuel had anointed, would have created a kind of mold for the next king. Look at Saul's description here:

> Kish had a son named Saul, as handsome a young man as could be found anywhere in Israel, and he was a head taller than anyone else. (1 Samuel 9:2)

Sound familiar?

Yes, the Lord's anointed prophet was about to fall into the trap of judging a book by its cover. Without the intervention of the Lord's voice—and Samuel's obedience to shake off his preconceived notions of what a king should look like—Samuel could have selected Saul 2.0 and saddled the nation with another bad king. Mind you, there had not been a king in Israel until Saul. God had made it clear that *he* wanted to be their King. Samuel would go on one by one with every son in the house, hearing from the Lord that none of them were chosen either. Could we blame Samuel for acting on his assumptions? Truth is, we very well might have done the same.

Identifiers vs. Identity

How do we escape this knee-jerk tendency toward visual judgment? How do we broaden our quick attempts to judge likability, competence, and other attributes based on how someone looks? It starts with acknowledging identifiers without tethering them to someone's identity as an individual.

I mentioned earlier that there's a big difference between identifiers and identity. Let's unpack that.

Remember, our identifiers are what we look like, and our identity is who we believe ourselves to be. The two concepts are linked, and we're in a constant battle to not let one dominate without discounting the influence of the other. Ultimately the way we think about this should point back to our God-made identity and the fact that the way he's created us to look aligns with who he has called us to be.

In case you need a refresher (don't sweat it if you do!), identifiers are things that we didn't get to choose for ourselves—our skin color, eye color, height, physical ability, age, gender, even the clothes our caregivers were able to afford during our younger years. We were dealt cards that we had no say in. Nonetheless, the Lord described our physical bodies as having value—because they're temples of the Holy Spirit: "Do you not know that your bodies are temples of the Holy Spirit, who is in you, whom you have received from God? You are not your own" (1 Corinthians 6:19).

Looks aren't everything, but the diverse multitude of humanity designed and created by God is something to be honored. Ultimately we are meant to embrace our physical attributes. After all, God acknowledges our physical bodies, with all their brokenness and beauty. He takes joy in what he made, even as he asks us to try to go beyond our limitations. A beautiful example of this was his call to Jeremiah:

> Before I formed you in the womb I knew you,
> and before you were born I consecrated you;
> I appointed you a prophet to the nations.
> (Jeremiah 1:5 ESV)

That's a mighty calling. But how did Jeremiah react?

"Alas, Sovereign LORD," I said, "I do not know how to speak; I am too young." But the LORD said to me, "Do not say, 'I am too young.' You must go to everyone I send you to and say whatever I command you. Do not be afraid of them, for I am with you and will rescue you," declares the LORD. (vv. 6–8)

When Jeremiah was chosen by the Lord, he was confused and felt disqualified because of his age. In other words, he resisted an assignment based on an identifier he could not change. But God looked past what Jeremiah couldn't change and spoke directly to his identity. Here is where we can see identity and identifiers intersecting. Identity has less to do with *what* we can see and more to do with *who* God has designed us to be.

Let's pause here and ask an important question: Have you allowed your opinions about yourself, others' opinions about you, or an overarching cultural narrative to give you an identity? These three groups are limited in perception. Whether it's you, someone else, or culture at large, no ID card on this earth can give you license to walk in the freedom of who you truly are.

Since that's the case, we need a better form of ID. Fortunately for us, God has been filling out our "ID forms" even before we got here. Meaning, God had a specific way he created all human beings. Remember? It's the *imago Dei*.

You might recall that *imago Dei* is a theological term translated from Latin as the "image of God," and it reflects what we see here in Genesis 1:27: "God created mankind in his own image, in the image of God he created them; male and female he created them." *Imago Dei* is the "likeness" of God that human beings bear because of the way he created us. It is something that, even after the fall, is part of our humanity. The *imago Dei* is our divine ID. No matter what our beliefs are, we resemble God differently than any other created life form. We are spiritual, rational, and creative, and within us is a desire to connect both vertically (with God) and horizontally (with one another).

So how do we live with this image in a healthy way? How do we use this divine ID?

Consider this: My driver's license specifies that I shouldn't operate a vehicle without corrective lenses and that I'm not allowed to drive a vehicle greater than twenty-six thousand pounds. So this ID allows me a certain level of freedom, but until I get that LASIK eye surgery (which terrifies me, by the way) and a Commercial Driver's License, I have to abide by the limitations on my ID for my own safety and the safety of those around me.

Similarly, if we don't know our God-given ID, then we run the risk of operating in life without a proper understanding of our limitations and stipulations (take a second to read 1 Corinthians 6:12, and you'll see what I mean). For example, God's Old Testament laws helped the Israelites keep their interpersonal relationships civil and their physical bodies healthy in the wilderness. And the laws also shaped them into a nation with a God-led identity. Likewise, God's commandments are still meant to guide us away from our weaknesses and away from our tendency to tear apart our relationships and corrupt our bodies through temptations.

However, unlike your ordinary ID, these particular limitations and stipulations don't change with corrective surgery or more knowledge; they change with a verification stamp of faith. That means the ID you possess may show characteristics that are deemed unworthy or disqualifying according to culture and society. Think of the Samaritan woman who had a bad reputation but became the first evangelist (John 4). Or the man with leprosy Jesus healed in the middle of a crowd, even though the man should've been far away from other people to begin with (Matthew 8). These people had stigmas that could have been debilitating and disqualifying, but these stigmas weren't big enough to prevent a touch from God. Our heavenly Miracle Worker often turns our most "disqualifying" pieces into our most effective tools for walking in great purpose!

Your God-given ID takes you beyond the physical and redeems your upbringing, background, and past. Just like the government insignia on any official license, you have the opportunity to be given authority to use this ID through the authority of the one who assigned it to you.

God Uses It All

So now that we know the difference between our identifiers and our identity, what do we make of it all? What do we do with this information?

Let me tell you this: your identifiers and your identity find themselves anchored in the person of Jesus. He is what living the *imago Dei* on earth should be, having been clothed in flesh like all humanity. In a later chapter we will examine the complexity that Jesus navigated and the road map he created for us all. But for now, I want to return our attention to Jeremiah.

As we saw earlier, God made an authoritative claim to Jeremiah: "Before I formed you in the womb I knew you" (Jeremiah 1:5). Jeremiah's calling as a prophet went beyond the scope of his physical existence. The same can be said of you. God knew his plans before you were born; he hasn't changed them due to any physical or cultural reality.

God continued by calling Jeremiah a prophet to the nations, and Jeremiah responded with a rebuttal, disqualifying himself due to his young age, inexperience, and lackluster public-speaking skills. This came from the limited understanding of what he assumed was required to be a prophet of the time. And he insisted he could not accept the title of "prophet" due to his lack of knowledge, skill, and experience.

Jeremiah's focus was on his physical, mental, and cultural limitations—his identifiers. But God shifted Jeremiah's priorities through one short conversation.

He called out Jeremiah's identity without dismissing his

age, boasting that, though human structures may be against Jeremiah due to his age, the Lord would empower and protect him on his assignment.

I love that God doesn't dismiss our identifiers. He doesn't diminish our realities. His will for our identity in him is to complement the identifiers we were born with. One of the most quotable scriptures in the Bible comes on the backside of one of the hardest realities that Jeremiah had to face. Acting as the prophet God called him to be, he told the people:

> This is what the LORD says: "When seventy years are completed for Babylon, I will come to you and fulfill my good promise to bring you back to this place. For I know the plans I have for you," declares the LORD, "plans to prosper you and not to harm you, plans to give you hope and a future." (Jeremiah 29:10–11)

Many of us love to quote Jeremiah 29:11, but the strength of this verse is found in its context. The Israelites were a minority people forced into a completely different culture, dominated by a foreign majority (Babylon) that was not friendly to their religious beliefs. But God went beyond this reality and reassured them that, though this time of exile would be long, his plans for them as his people would far outweigh the difficulties of their captivity.

I know that in my life, I've privately wrestled with questions about the way I look, the place I grew up, and the things I had or didn't have. When I've come to the Lord with these limitations and started to lean into the identity he has for me, I've gotten a new lens through which to view my life. I've been able to accept many of my experiences and situations and even see the Lord's plan that shaped me before I allowed him to take full control.

But I've got to be honest: the journey toward this realization was a tough one. Embracing our complexity is a complicated task, but if we begin with the Lord as our foundation, we can start to deconstruct our own misconceptions of ourselves. With him as our reference point, no matter what kind of picture is on our IDs, we can know that our *imago Dei* is unchangeable and filled with the possibility of God's calling for us on this earth. And in that calling, with that ID, we have access to more than we could have ever dreamed.

3

VISITOR'S PASS

The Origins of Belonging

"Alright, stand right there, and ... good," said the reception-
ist at the local high school I was visiting. It was like all the
other times I'd walked into a school over the previous decade
to speak to students at Bible studies or events. Before I could
talk to the students, I had to get a visitor's pass.

It's usually stamped with a time and a low-res, black-
and-white picture of my face. This pass becomes a form of
identification. It allows me access into the school, but it comes
with constraints. I can only go where the pass says I can go, do
what it says I'm there to do, and stay for an allotted amount
of time. I do not "belong" in these schools, but I am afforded

access due to my faith affiliation with the students who have invited me to attend.

This is a little like how society and cultures are constructed. Groups are organized into schools of identity. Whether it's a designation by race, ethnicity, politics, religion, gender, or culture, there are those who seem to belong and those who are given a visitor's pass. That means they've been given access by the gatekeeper of the group because they met the minimum requirement to be present. This visitor's pass gives them admission but with restrictions on where they can go, what they can do, and how long they can stay. In some cases, a shift in belief can grant them full access to the more ideological groups, as long as their convictions are in line with most of what the group believes. For example, those who lead in these types of groups are willing to tolerate those who don't neatly fit the group identity if it means more numbers, and oftentimes power is a numbers game. Once a group has gained power or prestige, those who are on the fringes can either completely conform to the group identity and work their way in, or if the group is based on an unchangeable fact like race, they have to be content with their partial acceptance with the knowledge they can never truly lead from within the group.

And then there are the cases where someone with a mixed heritage, a particular socioeconomic status, and other factors they cannot choose won't be allowed to ever become a full member of a group.

In my life's mixed contexts, I've often felt like I've been issued a visitor's pass. Like when I lived in an upper-middle-class neighborhood with a lower-middle-class budget and lifestyle. Or when I spent four days a week in my dad's inner-city immigrant church and five days a week rubbing elbows with peers from my affluent Anglo neighborhood. Or when I struggled with interpersonal relationships with homogeneous friend groups (whether Latino, white, or Black) where I was the obvious odd man out. For the most part, the name of the game in all these situations was "access"—who was in and who was out. Was I in? Or was I on the outside and only allowed momentary opportunities at certain times?

This happens to me on a micro level, for sure, but I'm far from the only person who experiences being forced to live within the confines of a group identity. In our society, once the parameters of *in* or *out* are established, usually by public and majority consensus, leaders emerge—the mouthpieces and greater contributors of the tribe rules. We decide who to trust, who to listen to. This usually comes in the form of electing those who embody the most prototypical components of the group at large.

The farther you are from the purest version of the group, the less weight your views or voice will have. In many situations, a mixed person's context slashes their chances of influence in half. When they add in their upbringing and culture, they may get a couple more points. But a lot of times, they may be demoted to having no authority. They can't participate; they're just allowed to be present. *Visitor's pass.*

All of a sudden, what claims to be a community of the like-minded—or at the least superficially similar—becomes a hierarchy that prioritizes pure-blooded over mixed. This applies not only to those of a racial or ethnic group but also to those of certain subcultures, socioeconomic statuses, and education levels.

School is a perfect example of this. If you walk into any high school cafeteria, you'll see that people typically shuffle themselves into groups. In your high school, maybe you had the nerds, jocks, musicians, and wannabe gangsters. I know mine did. Each group was composed of ethnic and racial groups that overlapped. In my case, it wasn't "cool" to be Latino/Black and be good in school. It was cool, however, to "thug out" and "act gangster," or to be an athlete. The more you fit with what the popular consensus was, the easier it was for you to make a home there.

Whatever groups you've encountered throughout your life, it's likely that at various points you've felt like a nomad, coming in at the lower levels—a guest—just as I have.

In that position we often seem to have two options: (1) continue to trudge through and force the round peg of our lives to fit in the square hole of a socially agreed-upon construct, or (2) depart unsatisfied, rejected, and lost. Both sound horrible. Both sound like an impossibly difficult way to live.

Instead, could we dare to believe there's a higher way, above what humans have created? A way that doesn't deny societal structures but instead allows room to go beyond those structures? Where we are not a victim of culture but rather a coproducer of an eternal reality that supersedes human-made boundaries and barriers?

Getting Boxed In

People will always want to put us in a box. And sometimes, we *want* to be in the box—in fact, we'll put ourselves there from time to time. When it comes to acceptance, we face boxes prescribed to us from the outside and boxes we create from within. From the outside, we have the broader culture and society trying to label or define us according to what is established by public consensus. These are what I call *group-limiting boxes* of society. Then there are the *self-limiting boxes* of the individual, which are hardest to discern and get out of. Self-limiting boxes are formed by our internal dialogue, by the way we talk about ourselves. They can be influenced by labels and comments from others, or by our own self-judgments, comparisons, and negativity. But here's the bad news: these types of pressure work together to form tidal waves that can wash away our self-esteem and drown out dreams and potential.

So being nomads, or people who don't necessarily fit in the "normal" boxes, how can we stand up against these pressures? We first need to understand what exactly we're dealing with—what our individual versions of these things are.

Let's start with group-limiting boxes. What are the toxic ways you might be interacting with your environment? How might society be robbing you of how you think about yourself and how you live the way God intended you to? Now, this doesn't necessarily have to involve society crushing us (though many times, it does). Oftentimes we can feel robbed of our

God-led identity simply when our sense of purpose is stifled by the boxes we find ourselves in.

Let's take a closer look at self-limiting boxes. Are there any Trojan horses that have infiltrated your mind and fostered doubt and fear? What paralyzing thoughts can you capture and offer to God, so he can replace them with truth?

Listen, these are tough questions that require some serious reflection and honesty. This discussion isn't meant to paint you as a victim of environment or a casualty of self-destruction. Actually, I'm trying to help with the opposite. I want to help illuminate the darkness that invades every one of our hearts so that we can equip ourselves to shine brightly, the way we're intended to.

To beat the lies of these boxes, we need awareness and insight *and* something else: a guide. A champion to help us. A King. One who can lead our nomadic existence through these dangers, because he doesn't just know the truth or the way to go—he *is* the truth, and he *is* the way. We need a King without borders.

A King Without Borders

The Romani people, known to the world by the name "gypsies," are nomadic. This group has no established home; their custom is to move from place to place with little to no attachment to wherever they settle. They make a quick entrance and exit, temporarily benefiting from a location, maybe getting food, shelter, governmental protection, and moderate weather.

It's estimated that there are twelve million Romani today, with about eight to ten million residing in Europe. Because of the lack of clarity of their history and oral tradition, and their mixing with other groups, a lot of details on their true ethnic identity are hard to distinguish, which contributes to their complex relationship with the nations they travel through. Locals wonder, *Who are these people?* And that's a hard question to answer.

Throughout their 1,500-year history, the Romani have had all sorts of encounters with the populations they've visited. Sometimes they enjoyed a king's watchful protection and the locals' hospitality. Other times they've faced ethnic and racial discrimination and forced assimilation, creating systemic barriers for the gypsy lifestyle.[1] They even became victims of the Nazi regime during World War II, when up to 1.5 million Romani perished in camps with the Jews.[2]

Now, why the deep dive into this informal nomadic nation? Because we can learn from these people who embody the idea of not truly belonging anywhere. They're constantly moving from place to place to sustain their lives and futures. Wherever they find themselves, people may accept or reject them, and they must choose how to respond.

You and I are not too different from this. It is possible you've felt like this in every stage of life, from childhood up until now, experiencing a group's limited acceptance or rejection time and again.

The Romani have proven to be masters at adapting to any nation they find themselves in. Throughout history they've fought for survival in countries that weren't their own and through wars they didn't start, yet they've never been counted among the nationals—even when nations have made concerted efforts to make this a reality. Through wars, crossing entire continents, and even landing overseas, the resilience of these people is world-renowned. Through all this they keep their own strong cultural identity while interacting with the people around them. Even if they speak the local language and exemplify the culture's traits, they'll never be considered native.

Tyson Fury, who is the self-proclaimed Gypsy King, is a two-time world heavyweight champion and lineal heavyweight champion in professional boxing. Though he is English, his heritage is Roma, a culture that would organize bare-knuckle boxing tournaments to crown the winners "King of the Gypsies." This was not a political title or even a form of nobility, but the embodiment of their toughness as a people. Interestingly, Tyson Fury has ancestors from both sides of his family who were boxing champions, people who were named King of the Gypsies.

So here is a people group who has been shaped by the trials of a tumultuous stack of centuries, and they've designated someone as embodying the best of their traits. Perhaps this is the type of king we need. One who has embodied our struggles, who has fought to earn the right to be the king of those who wander the earth. A champion.

Truth is, we are all nomads, even if we don't know it. We are eternal, spiritual beings in mortal flesh on earth for a finite amount of time. We're making our way through this broken world, trying our best not to break ourselves. Though we set up homes here, it won't be long before we move on.

Maybe at the core of our desire for acceptance is a desire to be who we truly were created to be and arrive where we ultimately belong—to be in heaven, our true home.

Maybe you feel the words of this old spiritual, like I do:

> *I'm just a poor wayfaring stranger*
> *Traveling through this world below*
> *There is no sickness, no toil or danger*
> *In that bright land to which I go*[3]

That could be our anthem as nomads. Until we get to that bright land in heaven, though, how do we find our way through earth?

In the book of Philippians, Paul described this space between now and then:

> Our citizenship is in heaven. And we eagerly await a Savior from there, the Lord Jesus Christ, who, by the power that enables him to bring everything under his control, will transform our lowly bodies so that they will be like his glorious body. (3:20–21)

Indeed, we all are visitors here, born into this world with a time frame. Jesus had the same parameters during his thirty-three years on earth. He made it clear that, though we ought to live our lives in service to the Lord, we also should keep our minds set on the reality of eternity. He said to his disciples,

> Do not let your hearts be troubled. You believe in God; believe also in me. My Father's house has many rooms; if that were not so, would I have told you that I am going there to prepare a place for you? And if I go and prepare a place for you, I will come back and take you to be with me that you also may be where I am. You know the way to the place where I am going. (John 14:1–4)

For those who don't feel like they have a place in this world, this promise hits deep.

Jesus was so intensely invested in his heavenly home that he experienced a type of homelessness on earth. "Foxes have dens and birds have nests, but the Son of Man has no place to lay his head," he said (Luke 9:58). Biblical scholar D. A. Carson wrote about this verse, "In the immediate context of Jesus' ministry, the saying does not mean that Jesus was penniless but homeless; the nature of his mission kept him on the move . . . and would keep his followers on the move."[4]

In this sense, Jesus extends an invitation to a journey, one that does not promise stability or even safety, but instead something much more satisfying: purpose. The motivation of true mission kept Christ from tethering to this temporal world. He invites us to do the same—to join him on a journey of accomplishing eternal purposes.

If we say yes to his invitation, we'll know who we are, even when we live on earth with visitor's passes. We'll remember the victory Christ gave us when he chose to fight against structures in culture and society. He'll become our Gypsy King. He'll win the battle on our behalves as the leader of the people with no home. He'll lead us through a world that tempts us to stake our claim in it and lures us to desire what is temporal instead of fixing our eyes on our eternal destination.

When you know who you belong to, you'll begin to see the labels others try to give you so that you'll belong. Only then can you fight back with the victory you've been given. Only then can you live outside the box.

Redefining Belonging

We're going to take another look at how we end up living within boxes and explore how our King can lead us away from them.

From the outside, group-identifying thoughts and beliefs such as, "We're not the kind of people who . . ." or "That's not for us" are often passed down through family, friends, and culture. From the inside, we carry our own judgment or prejudice toward others, which can come from our perceptions or preconceived notions of them. This is hard to admit, but honestly, we all do this in various ways and to different degrees. We use labels, we put people in boxes, and, in our worst moments, we judge: "Those people are ignorant, dangerous, uptight, bigots, lazy, rude." These types of beliefs or assumptions are often not merited or driven by experience; they're usually oversimplified attempts to understand who people are through easy categorization.

These types of prejudice can come in the form of racism, classism, and other judgments based on someone's appearance, speech, or dress. It's a shortcut to defining someone's belonging. And it usually lands someone with a visitor's pass, a label with constraints on where they can belong and what they can do.

Listen closely when I say this: prejudice not only compels us to elevate or idolize someone we've made into the standard of success; it also allows us to devalue or dehumanize another human being. That is frightening. And that kind of dehumanization is at the root of so much evil we've seen throughout history. Whenever a group has been ostracized, oppressed, or killed, you see labels attached to them—labels that devalue their identity and signify that they don't belong. It's straight out of the devil's playbook.

And that's why we should keep this in mind: the Lord has revealed that, regardless of the evils established, promoted, and perpetuated by humans (those prejudices and judgments), our true Enemy is an invisible one. As a matter of fact, I often say, "If you can see them, they are not your enemy." Here's how Paul put it: "Our struggle is not against flesh and blood, but against the rulers, against the authorities, against the powers of this dark world and against the spiritual forces of evil in the heavenly realms" (Ephesians 6:12). His words remind us that there's a bigger story at play when you're hit with a label that's not really you. Someone is trying to take away your true identity. And that someone is the enemy of Christ.

Hear this: The basis of your identity is not founded on anything outside of Christ. In his holiness and love, he guides our interactions, attitudes, and beliefs about others. And if that's not happening in our society, it's time for us to examine whether we view ourselves and others through the lens of Christ or the lens of culture. Whether we're allowing the "powers of this dark world" to take the lead.

So let's get introspective. What have we allowed to shape our worldviews? And how has that affected our interactions with the world? Many groups can make up the intricate mosaic of our identity. And just like making an actual mosaic, some colors, shapes, and patterns can be more dominant at times than others. When this happens, it can give us identity whiplash—even an identity crisis—when we can't back up and see how these intricate pieces work together to make a beautiful whole work of art.

Hopefully, as we determine where we can detach unhealthy beliefs from groupthink, we can drop our labels, break down our boxes, and gain space. Space to give to the Lord, so he can reconstruct our views and help us create a beautiful mosaic within that shows his purpose for our lives.

What About Racism?

In all this talk about labels, it's important to take a moment to recognize that racism is a unique issue and that moving away from labels doesn't mean we can minimize or avoid it. Racism is real, and it is one of the ugliest forms of putting people in a box. I may have lost some people here, but that's alright. This is, in part, why it's so important to talk about this subject. Let's dig in a bit so we know how to do just that. The word *racism* is defined by the *Merriam-Webster* dictionary as "a belief that race is a fundamental determinant of human traits and capacities and that racial differences produce an inherent superiority of a particular race."[5]

Although racism is typically categorized as a prejudice of the dominant group of a culture toward the less dominant one, this definition doesn't exclude anyone from being racist. Anyone from any background can be racist, and with the changing demographics of the United States projected to become a majority "minority" nation by 2045,[6] we cannot afford to limit this definition. In about a hundred years, the Hispanic/Latino population may become the dominant group. If we do one day outnumber other groups, it would pain me to see us also discriminate against others that don't look, sound, or think like us.

Many think that ignoring the color of people is the answer to solving racism. Some are asking, "Why should we talk about race at all? Shouldn't we be busting through our labels every which way?" I hear you. But instead of skirting the issue, I think it's more important—and more effective at "busting those labels"—to talk about it. Let's focus on some points that'll help us engage in better conversations about racism and diversity.

1. Diversity Is Our Reality

In the United States, all 190 nations of the world are represented. Isn't that crazy? But here's something else: digital globalization, which makes us more connected than ever, is tearing down the walls of homogeneous communities and forcing people to confront their prejudices and ignorance like never before.

Here's the biggest truth we have to face: we live in a fallen world. Culture has grappled with the topic of race, especially in America, for centuries. If we wish to create cultural change, we must be agents of redemption in the midst of culture, not wait for culture to change by osmosis. If we don't engage culture, we'll perpetuate culture. One of my mentors, Rev. Samuel Rodriguez, stated it this way during a speech at Liberty University: "Today's complacency is tomorrow's captivity."[7] In other words, the gospel is designed to work in the offensive position: for advancement and expansion. Jesus stated that it is the devil's place to be on defense, with gates to protect his interests and keep the captives bound:

> Jesus replied, "Blessed are you, Simon son of Jonah, for this was not revealed to you by flesh and blood, but by my Father in heaven. And I tell you that you are Peter, and on this rock I will build my church, and the gates of Hades will not overcome it." (Matthew 16:17–18)

If we want to participate in the gospel's offensive work and speak on cultural topics, we have to use the language of the conversation. Only then can we move the conversation into a healthier place. For example, you may think that "race" is a social construct and that the Bible does not refer to people groups as "races." I agree—but I still use that term to engage in the cultural conversation because I want to make every effort to reach someone and, hopefully, deepen their understanding. And in order to help someone understand where I'm coming from more effectively, it's a lot easier to use language they're familiar with. Let's not be afraid to use terms that can feel loaded at times, given where they're spoken and who's speaking them, and watch the way they're used when boxing in or labeling human beings.

2. The Bible Talks About Diversity

Are race and ethnicity important to talk about? The Bible tells me yes. It explicitly talks about racial and ethnic diversity in many places. First, we see the Table of Nations in Genesis 10, where people "spread out into their territories by their clans within their nations, each with its own language" (v. 5). Then, in the beginning of civilization, at the Tower of Babel and the scattering of all people with different languages and cultures (Genesis 11), we see a catalyst of ethnic diversity. Humans attempted to gain a name for themselves by building a tower that would reach heaven, forsaking the plan of God for many to spread throughout the world and take dominion. Later, the

Spirit of God fell on the people and created many languages among them, which caused the people to stop their building and scatter far and wide.

Those are just a few mentions—the list goes on. God promised Abraham he would become the father of many (diverse) nations, and God launched a redemptive plan to bring these distinctive people groups back together (Genesis 12).

Moses led a mixed multitude in his exodus from Egypt. The Lord made a covenant of generosity to sojourners (Exodus 12).

Jesus himself was of mixed heritage, and his ministry was diverse among Jews, Samaritans, and Romans (we will cover this in detail in a later chapter).

Peter had a vision that led him on a mission to the Gentiles, a group considered outside Jewish holiness (Acts 10).

The apostle Paul commissioned a Gentile harvest (Acts 22:21), and John recorded a vision in the book of Revelation about all people distinct in their ethnicity, tribe, and language (7:9).

If you are looking for examples of racial and ethnic diversity in the Bible, you have plenty to choose from. If it's important enough to be in God's story of humanity from the beginning, it's important to talk about now as well.

3. Unity Is Possible

Jesus showed in his "high priestly prayer" (John 17) that his heart for his people is restoration and unity: "[I pray] that all of them may be one, Father, just as you are in me and I am in you.

May they also be in us so that the world may believe that you have sent me" (v. 21). That tells us it's possible, and it's Jesus' goal for us—the priority of our King without borders.

But this biblical unity is an unnatural posture for humans. It requires supernatural transformation. To be as one, we must turn to heaven for help. Jesus showed us how—through prayer. Because unity doesn't just happen by osmosis, we have to keep talking about it, praying about it, pursuing it. We have to keep "unboxing."

4. We're Eternal People

Last, why should we be talking about race? Because what we look like, who we came from, and how we speak is what we get to take into eternity with us. Revelation 7:9 gives us a picture of heaven: "Before me was a great multitude that no one could count, from every nation, tribe, people and language, standing before the throne and before the Lamb. They were wearing white robes and were holding palm branches in their hands."

You probably remember the song in children's church: "Red and yellow, black and white. They are precious in his sight. Jesus loves the little children of the world." You may even be inclined to agree with this oversimplified verse of a children's song in conjunction with the verse we just read in Revelation. But this begs the question: Are there any groups that my Christian worldview won't make room for in heaven?

This question has gotten very personal for me—and

uncovered an issue I think a lot of people don't consider. When God says "every nation," he really means *every* nation. Regardless of past tragedies, tyranny, and turmoil, no nation is exempt from the grace that saves souls. No geopolitical ideology should keep us from believing that every nation can be reached and saved. So, with intentionality, we must fight to set our hearts on God's will for the future, on the reality that nations will one day come together in Christ and spend eternity as one family.

Regaining Human Dignity in a Divisive Conversation

My wife, Alexis, is a second-generation Christian Palestinian American.

Before I met her, I had a limited understanding of the Palestinian people. Given my Latino heritage, Pentecostal Christian upbringing, and education in the South, all I knew about the Palestinian-Israeli conflict I learned in these contexts and, in many ways, had adopted a surface-level understanding as a firm belief in what was happening there.

I recall a moment when a Latin American friend asked if I had converted my wife or if she had converted before meeting me. He didn't even mention the word *Muslim*, but I asked if that was what he meant, and he said yes. I then, as gracefully as I could, relayed to him that her family had been Christians longer than Christianity had been in the Americas. It might sound petty, but I felt defensive in that moment as I addressed the misconceptions about my wife and her people and the way they've all been issued visitor's passes in a place they should have felt at home.

I met Alexis in 2014, and we got married in 2017. After years of getting to know her, falling in love, and building relationships with her family members from the States and Palestine, my eyes were opened not just to the identity of the Palestinian people but to God's active work in and among them. I was able to shed the demonization of a people group I'd been taught to fear and, in some ways, hate because of their supposed obstruction of God's will to restore Israel.

It didn't help when the media's portrayal of extremist groups like Hamas started using the blanket term *Arab*. My wife is half Arab. My kids are one-quarter Arab. *Arab* has so much more meaning than the label it has been reduced to—especially when it's used to discount someone's place in God's plan.

When we put labels and limitations on people groups, when we, through our ignorance and distance, force them into a box, we can end up with harmful language and even destructive actions against others. My wife has had some difficult moments with Christians in the States and with Jews in Israel (you can hear her share more about this in podcast interviews).[8] Her family members in Beit Sahour, Palestine, have many stories of bearing the brunt of discrimination.

But be assured, God is at work within that community. I've had the privilege to talk with her grandmother who still lives there. She is a woman of faith and a minister in her own right who hears from the Holy Spirit. She has shared stories of the Holy Spirit waking her up in the middle of the night with visions and dreams that helped her and her family navigate the violence of the 1980s and '90s in their part of Palestine. Not only her but other Palestinian Christians are doing incredible ministry in reconciling Muslims, Jews, and Christians.

In some places I've been, the term *Palestinian Christian* or *Christian Arab* would have been treated like an oxymoron. Even so, it's true. We are more than our labels, and God works beyond them.

We're eternal people with God-designed distinctions, and our King has made room for every nation in his glorious heaven. Despite histories, media coverage, controversy, and geopolitical turmoil, he did not shy away from making his heavenly home big enough for any and every person to come in. The beauty of God in the creation of humanity is the wealth of its diversity, manifested through its people, with both the physical features we were born with and the times and culture we were born into. God seems to care a lot about both of these realities and has chosen to bring that complexity to eternity. He has deliberately gifted each of us with our distinctions, which proves their importance.

Talking about race isn't a distraction. It's merely the first step toward the reconciliation of all people to one another, through the reconciliation of God and humanity bought by Christ's blood. Following our mobile, versatile King without borders, we need to be walking with one another into our respective worlds, sharing our stories and culture, and celebrating our distinctions while being unified as one people through Christ's blood. That's our goal. And as we celebrate, travel, and experience life with one another, we all can take off our visitor's passes. Because we all belong in the kingdom of God.

So if you feel like you've been issued a visitor's pass to certain groups and systems, and even if you've put yourself in that category, I invite you to unclip it from your jacket. You may be made to feel like an outsider in certain places, but when you open your eyes to a wider world—a world where we all belong—you'll know you have a place. This is a world where, instead of being pressured to conform to human categories, we follow a King without borders who leads us toward a beautiful future. And on that journey, we experience the power of living in our real identities.

4

BREAKING OUT
OF THE BOX

Culture Traps: Group Limitations

"Do you feel like you're "part of the system"? Or is "the system" getting you down? Have you ever felt like you've taken the red pill in *The Matrix* and now you're falling down the rabbit hole toward a place constructed to typecast you into a prebuilt dystopia?

Okay, that sounded a little intense. But there's some preprogramming built into the systems of this world, implemented *way* before we got here, that, if we're not careful, may lull us to sleep in its rhythmic tick of trends and tragedies.

This is the danger of our systems: we identify with them.

Sometimes way too much. In *social* systems within the US, we identify with groups according to race and ethnicity, as we've been discussing. In our *economic* systems, we identify with a certain class or income level. In our *religious* systems, we identify with our flavor of faith. In our *political* systems, we identify with a party or a certain set of ideals. And sure, these systems inform how we see ourselves and other people—that's natural. But again, if we overidentify with groups constructed by humans, they begin to fail us and keep us apart.

We need to open our eyes to these groups, how they function in our lives, and the pressure they put on us. We need to regain a vision of societal structures that correspond with a world that is much more complex than our systems and groups would have us think. Let's look at some of the divisions we deal with and how the group-limiting thoughts and pressures that come from them affect us. Only then can we sort out the difference between humanity's way and God's way.

Socioeconomic Boxes: The Haves and the Have-Nots

"America is a third world country in a Gucci belt."[1]

I came across this statement in a Tweet and thought it reflected how frustration in America is reaching all-time highs. During the tensions and tragedies of 2020, many people woke up to the fact that the rhetoric touted by leadership from all sides seemed hollow and empty. It was as if the name of our nation and the pride of our people was just a superficial cloak covering the systemic brokenness that had been created by broken people.

No matter how good the ideal we hold when we construct and reconstruct our nation, it seems like America continues to be the land where wealth and poverty walk hand in hand. How has this happened? It's as if the moment we identify with what we have, we begin to relate to others through the framework of the "haves" and "have-nots."

Those who "have" might think the system works great, saying things like, "The American Dream should work for everyone, and if it doesn't, it's their fault." Those who "have not" might say, "It doesn't work, and it's their fault." With both systemic and human brokenness, the tendency to lean toward a hierarchy defined by materialism and wealth is inevitable. Good intentions aren't enough because good intentions are not the problem; sin is.

You've probably heard the phrase "The road to hell is paved with good intentions." J. Davila-Ashcraft, an Anglican priest, theologian, and apologist, considered the phrase with a Christian perspective and said, "The road to hell is not really paved with good intentions, but with sin. It is a sinful heart that seeks to manipulate our good intentions, and we are all sinners."[2]

Whatever our socioeconomic reality, there is no amount of good intention, power, or resource that can save us from a corrupted flesh that needs the crucifixion in order to be raised to new life. Jesus, in his scolding rebuke to the Pharisees,

highlighted what can happen to even the most devout followers of God if they're not careful:

> Woe to you, teachers of the law and Pharisees, you hypo-
> crites! You are like whitewashed tombs, which look beautiful
> on the outside but on the inside are full of the bones of the
> dead and everything unclean. In the same way, on the out-
> side you appear to people as righteous but on the inside you
> are full of hypocrisy and wickedness. (Matthew 23:27–28)

As you can see the original "Gucci belt" clapback was from
Christ. Cold. But true. Elitism can creep into our benevolence
to the point that we perpetuate inequality, poverty, and harm
in the name of God.

Before we move on, I want to talk about what might be
the most misquoted and taken-out-of-context scripture I've
heard (outside of Philippians 4:13—"I can do all this through
[Christ] who gives me strength"—as a "gym" scripture, because
your hamstrings don't agree that you can lift all things through
Christ who strengthens you!). It's 1 Timothy 6:10: "The *love*
of money is a root of all kinds of evil. Some people, eager for
money, have wandered from the faith and pierced themselves
with many griefs" (emphasis added). People constantly omit
a highly significant word from the scripture's message and
assume that *money* is the root of all evil. But that's not what it
says. Money in and of itself is not the root of evil; the *love* of
money is.

A similar message is found in Jesus' words: "Do not store

up for yourselves treasures on earth. . . . But store up for your-selves treasures in heaven. . . . No one can serve two masters. Either you will hate the one and love the other, or you will be devoted to the one and despise the other. You cannot serve both God and money" (Matthew 6:19–20, 24). This scripture is so important when we discuss our relationship with money and status, because the pursuit of the American Dream and the human desire to have more and more material wealth has robbed many from understanding spiritual truths. They place themselves above some people and attempt to work their way to be above others. Jesus in his wisdom pointed his followers to what matters most; he told them to store up true treasures above, not to toil for lesser treasures here on earth.

Is this to say that we should be poor for the Lord? Not at all. Nor do I believe that Jesus' goal is to make us all rich. Jesus knows that if we don't allow him to be our master, then what we own will be the master over us. The dangers of allowing our possessions to possess us are gravely underrated and not emphasized nearly enough in our culture today. Tethering all that we have to God and not to ourselves is the beginning of being liberated from a mentality of what is "mine" and what is "theirs."

Sometimes our possessions and the status they give us can start to dominate the way we operate in life and society. So we always need to keep the right priorities. If we allow our socio-economic status to become a definitive identity we pursue or flaunt, we run the risk of losing what's most important in life and even—according to Jesus—losing our souls. "What good is it for someone to gain the whole world, yet forfeit their soul?" he said (Mark 8:36), and also, "Seek first his kingdom and his righteousness, and all these things will be given to you as well" (Matthew 6:33).

In fact, Jesus repeatedly put money and possessions in their place: "Indeed, it is easier for a camel to go through the eye of a needle than for someone who is rich to enter the kingdom of God" (Luke 18:25). It is not impossible for a rich man to enter into the kingdom of heaven, but the parable of the seeds shows us why it would be so difficult: "The seed falling among the thorns refers to someone who hears the word, but the worries of this life and the deceitfulness of wealth choke the word, making it unfruitful" (Matthew 13:22).

We can take it straight from Jesus' mouth: wealth can be deceitful, so it's a dangerous place to rest our identities.

Poverty Tourism

This type of group-limiting thought process—the "deceitfulness of wealth"—doesn't sink its talons into the psyche of only those who are cartoonishly greedy, like a Scrooge of some sort, but also into those who enjoy viewing themselves as financially benevolent, which can veer into giving from a posture of superiority. Sometimes this comes in the form of an American twentysomething spending a week in Africa primarily to use their social media posts to elevate their standing with their peer group and religious affiliates. Parody Instagram accounts like @BarbieSavior critique this type of culture, which has turned mission trips into vacations with a social service add-on.

Any time we serve someone, especially those in need, we run the risk of starting to view ourselves as not just more fortunate but superior in morality and material wealth. We also can turn those who are in need into DIY projects. We may dehumanize those who "need" us because we believe we can do the saving.

In their book, *When Helping Hurts: How to Alleviate Poverty Without Hurting the Poor . . . and Yourself*, Covenant College community development professor Steve Corbett and his coauthor, Brian Fikkert, an economics professor at the school, lay this out perfectly: *"Until we embrace our mutual brokenness, our work with low-income people is likely to do far more harm than good.* . . . I sometimes unintentionally reduce poor people to objects that I use to fulfill my own need to accomplish something. . . . 'I am not okay; and you are not okay. But Jesus can fix us both.'"[3]

I have been disturbed to realize how often I can put on a "savior" or "messiah" complex (wow—it feels awful just writing that). It's something that is easily accepted in the minds of believers as a source of zeal toward a godly mission—"saving" people from their poverty, addiction, or sinful situation. The issue with this is that we have no right to be doing any saving because we ourselves need to be saved.

In her book *Accidental Saints: Finding God in All the Wrong People*, pastor and theologian Nadia Bolz-Weber stated:

> While we as people of God are certainly called to feed the hungry and clothe the naked, that whole "we're blessed to be a blessing" thing can still be kind of dangerous. It can be dangerous when we self-importantly place ourselves above the world, waiting to descend on those below so we can be the "blessing" they've been waiting for, like it or not.[4]

The reality is this: though the title "Christian" comes from the Greek word *Christianos*, meaning "little Christ," we are not equals with Christ; we live in full submission to him. This allows his life to flow in and through us, guiding and empowering how we love and serve one another. As Paul said, "I have been crucified with Christ and I no longer live, but Christ lives in me. The life I now live in the body, I live by faith in the Son of God, who loved me and gave himself for me" (Galatians 2:20). So if "America is a third world country with a Gucci belt," then a Christian living without Christ and full submission to his will is a dead corpse with a Gucci belt, well-dressed with no life in him. Only Christ can provide a guiding light; money, material wealth, and status cannot. When it comes to group-limiting boxes in our world that focus on one's socioeconomic status, Jesus leads us to look beyond the haves and have-nots to discover that all we have is in him.

Religious Boxes: Holy Rollers vs. High Church

Growing up as a Pentecostal, I didn't find it too hard to wade through the waters of my Christianity. One reason was because we were radically expressive in proclaiming the Word and demonstrating the acts of the disciples. I accepted the call of God on my life at the age of sixteen. As a good Pentecostal, I had accepted Christ probably a thousand times up until that point, and I'm sure several ministers counted every one of my commitments as a salvation tally mark for their reports.

On the day I accepted Christ wholly and fully, it was like no other day. Broken and empty, I gave Jesus one last shot, and three hours later at the altar, with snot and tears drying up, I stood up and started walking back to my seat. My youth pastor quickly approached me and handed me a piece of paper—a Bible study sheet. It had a clear outline of a Bible lesson that was meant for someone to study, then teach. He said that if I was serious about giving my life to the Lord in this moment, I should go and tell my friends at school about my faith.

And that's exactly what I did. I started a Bible study, invited eight friends, and stumbled through a teaching on John 15 (yeah, that's right, it was so bad I remember what I taught almost two decades later). None of them came back. But with a whole lot of prayer and faith, things started changing. Within two and a half years, a few friends and I saw God use us to grow a small group of radical teenagers into a movement on our high school campus numbering in the hundreds.

During this time, I didn't know much, but I believed God. I hadn't read a lot of the Bible until I started this Bible study, but I believed God. I never prayed beyond mealtimes and bedtimes until that point, but I believed God.

When I say, "I believed God," I mean that I believed his Word. While the nature of Pentecostal, charismatic, and Spirit-empowered movements is laced with the supernatural, loudness, and at times controversial means of demonstration, I didn't recognize or carry that burden. I had heard my father use the old-time phrase "Holy Rollers" to explain the way others viewed our group, but this label just kind of fell off me. Why? Because I believed God.

Today, having worked nationally and globally with ecumenical networks (representing a number of different Christian churches) and having friends and family in a range of affiliations, I have grown to appreciate the diversity of expression in the body of Christ. I can, however, attest to the division that still persists in the church body. I still claim Pentecostalism as my personal Christian affiliation, even as I see some people hesitate to embrace my tradition as equal to their own. There are jabs here and there about my tradition, whether it's our lack of order, lack of biblical knowledge, or fledgling line of theologians. I am not here to argue these points. But if we want to move forward as the church Christ died for and established, we need to hold unity in the highest regard.

As borders between groups start to fall because of a growing wave of secularism and because young people of different ideological and belief groups are starting to cross-pollinate with one another, we will increasingly find ourselves inter-secting. The worst thing we can do is allow our labels and associations within the body of Christ to dismiss or omit others. This type of thinking doesn't build the body; it's like a cancer within the body. It causes us to be malformed and sick from the inside, eating away at ourselves.

When Paul heard about division in the Corinthian church, he pointed out how senseless it was:

> Some from Chloe's household have informed me that there are quarrels among you. . . . One of you says, "I follow Paul"; another, "I follow Apollos"; another, "I follow Cephas"; still another, "I follow Christ." Is Christ divided? Was Paul cru-cified for you? Were you baptized in the name of Paul?
> (1 Corinthians 1:11–13)

Divisions in the body are not new. They have always been a battle for the believer. Celebrity Christianity isn't new either. There have always been people whom God uses publicly, and followers fall into the trap of prioritizing a personal affiliation with a leader above their allegiance to Christ. Sometimes, it's affiliations like these that prevent unity with one another.

Your identity should not be found in your denomination affiliation, how cool your pastor is, whether you have free cof-fee in your church's lobby, or even the things your church does in the community. Our whole allegiance is to Christ. From this place we can serve our local church and be a healthy part of the capital C Church in the world. This belief is what I held when

I was sixteen, and and through the years I have had to fight to make sure my belief in God always superseded the temptation to champion my denominational tribe over another.

My invitation to you is to not board yourself up in a box of tertiary beliefs held by any faction of Christianity. Don't let differing views on worship style, drinking, hair color, and school choice prompt you to hurl insults and stones. Instead, make the essentials of Christianity your foundation—the authority of the Bible; the deity of Christ; the Trinity; the birth, death, and resurrection of Jesus; and salvation through Jesus by faith through grace.

In an effort to emphasize unity of the body of Christ, Paul made it plain to us how we should love one another. He was writing to believers in Ephesus, a diverse place at the time, with rivaling ministries. They needed unity, and Paul guided them:

> Be completely humble and gentle; be patient, bearing with one another in love. Make every effort to keep the unity of the Spirit through the bond of peace. There is one body and one Spirit, just as you were called to one hope when you were called; one Lord, one faith, one baptism; one God and Father of all, who is over all and through all and in all. (Ephesians 4:2–6)

"Make every effort." That means unity can sometimes be a labor of love. We have to choose to love our brothers and sisters, regardless of our agreement or disagreement on the peripheral issues, and remember Jesus' prayer that we would be one so the world would come to know him. We need to break out of our religious boxes to make that happen.

Political Boxes: "Not My President"

On social media, we have seen people polarize and radicalize in their viewpoints at an alarming rate. Throughout the last several election cycles, the split between both major political parties has grown larger and larger. In 2017, Pew research found that "eighty percent of Americans today feel unfavorable toward their partisan foes, and the portion feeling *very* unfavorable has nearly tripled since 1994."[5]

During the election of President Trump, a phrase said commonly among his political critics was, "Not my president." When President Biden was elected, the echo of "Not my president" persisted among the new president's detractors.

Apart from a few radicals, the longing for capable and just leadership is universal. Political strife is not new. But even if we don't agree with the policies and politicians of the day, we will always be subject to some form of governance or leadership here on earth (even Jesus admitted as much—we'll talk about this more in a minute).

As citizens of heaven who live in this world, I don't think we should ignore the relevant issues of the day, because policy affects other people, whether they live across the street or across the country. And we're supposed to love other people, right?

So whether you're fighting for your nation in your prayer closet or picketing on Capitol Hill, your faith can definitely inform your political beliefs and the way you carry them out. But hear me, friend: it's dangerous to let a political or ideological group become your identity. If someone asked you about it, you probably wouldn't say that your political affiliation *is* your identity, or even a big part of it. You probably didn't make a conscious decision. Maybe you're passionate to bring about a change you wish to see, something you firmly believe would help someone else and make the world a better place. But here's why going all in and putting all your chips on a political party or ideological group is risky: in some way, every government structure is broken because broken people constructed them.

Throughout the history of humanity, there has been a fight for power. That's where the word *politics* comes from. The *Merriam-Webster* dictionary defines the word as "the art or science concerned with winning and holding control over a government."[6] It isn't inherently evil for people to organize themselves into towns, cities, or countries; structure, governance, and order can help societies flourish, after all. But without God, without his love for people underwriting the policies and laws that shape a group of people, humanity has the proclivity to act on all sorts of evil.

So what do rhetoric and policies from groups without God in the mix sound like? What do they look like? Often you find a lust for power that is laced with pride. This is the root of it all, and as we all know, roots are the part of the thing we can't see. Those things that are being organized and grown in our society have the potential to poison a generation with the fruit of rebellion, violence, bitterness, and all manner of evil that causes people to indulge their sinful nature while justifying the oppression—and at the most extreme, termination—of any and all groups that threaten the power they possess. This is no way to live. Yet this is the ultimate plan of the devil for humanity. In John 10:10 Jesus stated, "The thief comes only to steal and kill and destroy." I'm glad Jesus didn't end there but instead added, "I have come that they may have life, and have it to the full." Groups without God are just tools for the Enemy to bring about the total ruin of all people.

So don't forget: we need to hold loosely any identity tied to a group we are affiliated with, because at the end of the day, we have a higher identity as citizens of heaven.

Broken People and Broken Systems

Remember Samuel, the prophet who went looking for a king? He tried to judge a book by its cover but ended up with David, the unconventional choice. That all started when the people demanded a king.

The Bible often talks about the dangers of human governance. God warned the people of Israel when they longed to be led traditionally like the kingdoms surrounding them:

The LORD told [Samuel]: "Listen to all that the people are saying to you; it is not you they have rejected, but they have rejected me as their king. As they have done from the day I brought them up out of Egypt until this day, forsaking me and serving other gods, so they are doing to you. Now listen to them; but warn them solemnly and let them know what the king who will reign over them will claim as his rights." (1 Samuel 8:7–9)

Samuel continued with the command the Lord gave him. He pulled no punches as he warned the people of all the harm that would come from being ruled this way. But nevertheless, the Israelites insisted:

The people refused to listen to Samuel. "No!" they said. "We want a king over us. Then we will be like all the other nations, with a king to lead us and to go out before us and fight our battles." When Samuel heard all that the people said, he repeated it before the LORD. The LORD answered, "Listen to them and give them a king." (vv. 19–22)

The rest is history. Only a handful of Israel's kings would be considered just in the Lord's eyes, but even *they* left a trail of tragedies and mistakes along the way. And everyone else? They left some of the worst atrocities the nation had ever experienced in their wakes. This caused the people to suffer in exile (remember the famous exile to Babylon?).

Honestly, it's not that much different today. Broken people

create broken systems that still fall painfully short of the flourishing God wants for all of his children. I don't want to discount the moments of progress humanity has achieved, but think about how much bloodshed and injustice still occur today. Simply put, people make bad rulers, and no government or ideology group is perfect. We shouldn't be naive enough to believe that the ultimate solution for a broken humanity is to find the right human leader. The solution is to pray that the God who has the ability to change hearts would change ours, and pray that he would reign in the hearts of our leaders.

Paul had this to say on the topic:

> I urge, then, first of all, that petitions, prayers, intercession and thanksgiving be made for all people—for kings and all those in authority, that we may live peaceful and quiet lives in all godliness and holiness. This is good, and pleases God our Savior, who wants all people to be saved and to come to a knowledge of the truth. (1 Timothy 2:1–4)

And shouldn't that be our goal as well?

Belonging to His Kingdom

When Christ came to earth and ushered in a new humanity through his life, death, and resurrection, he brought with him a new way to live, a new kingdom with a new set of values flowing from the greatest power. God began manifesting himself through believers as he filled them with the Holy Spirit. This kingdom is not to be confused with any empire or government controlled by humans, even "virtuous" ones. This kingdom is governed by the Creator of all things, perfect in love, mercy, and justice.

This King leads his people to view power as a tool to redeem a broken world. His nation has no borders of politics, ethnicity, race, gender, upbringing, or socioeconomic status. It is open to all, and the King accepts people as they arrive.

To this end, the promise of his kingdom is not the freedom to do what one sees fit but rather to submit to a beautiful existence that far exceeds any purpose a group could give and any wisdom a human could offer. Within this framework we can lay down our ideologies of nationalism and ethnocentrism.

Nationalism is dangerous because we can hold the pride of our nation as something sacred enough to intertwine with our faith in the divine. We can end up with a tangled view of Christ and culture that produces beliefs that do not serve the kingdom or the mission of the church.

Ethnocentrism means you hold your ethnic makeup above others', isolating and emphasizing a standard that exists in your ethnic group. This creates a barrier to seeing God's work and blessing flowing through other ethnicities around us. Instead, we can lay down our desire for vengeful justice and warped exclusivism, and allow the character of our King to guide how we live and treat others.

After all, we "are no longer foreigners and strangers, but fellow citizens with God's people and also members of his household, built on the foundation of the apostles and prophets, with Christ Jesus himself as the chief cornerstone" (Ephesians 2:19–20).

As members of God's kingdom, it might be easy to say, "Well, I'll just ignore the actions and decisions of those in charge here on earth. All of this is fleeting, anyway." But the truth is, our interactions with public policy are part of our responsibilities as believers. Jesus alluded to this balance when speaking with the religious leaders in Matthew 22:15–22. We can infer that Jesus supported paying taxes when he took a coin with Caesar's image on it and said, "Give back to Caesar what is Caesar's, and to God what is God's" (v. 21).

This passage implies that Jesus stayed in line with governmental laws of the time while also staying true to his *imago Dei* identity. We can try to follow his example. If we are supposed to give to our earthly leaders what's made in their image, like Caesar's coin, then we're also compelled to give God what's made in *his* image—ourselves. It's a dual reality we live in. And so we walk through our earthly situations guided by our eternal destiny.

We all are influenced by the boxes we check, whether it's our incomes, religious affiliations, politics, or something else. Wherever we are on the spectrum of "belonging" in a group, we must remember that we first belong to God. That will make navigating our groups with compassion, authenticity, and growth-mindedness possible.

But just as we feel pressure from outside to fit a certain mold, we face pressure from within. That's what we'll talk about next.

5

BUILDING YOUR OWN BOX

The Danger of a Caricature Complex

I grew up playing the Nintendo 64. There was nothing quite like the moment I saw the first commercial for *Super Smash Bros.*, a battle-based game that pitted your favorite Nintendo characters against one another. You could bring in Mario, Donkey Kong, Samus, Kirby, or my all-time favorite, Pikachu, who to this day is my go-to character in *Super Smash*, no matter the iteration of the game.

Every character has its specialty, and with the right person wielding their special attacks, some of the characters are nigh unbeatable. That's both the joy and grief of fight-based video games—the combination of a player's proficiency and a character's abilities. The right character in the wrong hands can lead to a loss, and vice versa; if you have a weak character in the hands of a good player, you decrease your opponent's chances to exploit the character's weakness. Some character matchups are "broken" in the sense that players can successfully spam one button that causes the character to repeat the same move, catching an opponent in an unescapable attack. This proves effective sometimes. With some opponents you might get short-term success spamming the one effective move of your character, but when a real challenger arises, they can counter the move—and you'll be dead in the water.

This "spamming" move is what you might do if one dimension of your life is working successfully. You may have a go-to persona that charms people, helps you get ahead socially, and creates new opportunities for you. But this persona is not who you are. It's a move you exploit in order to reduce conflict and easily move through relationships. Basically, your character isn't authentic; you're a caricature of only a small part of who you are. You might suppress what you consider high-risk qualities, like a sense of humor or an accent, or project false emotions instead of vulnerability in order to coexist with people.

As a minority in majority Anglo contexts in the US, I have felt the pressure to be uber-Latino. Perhaps this reflex came from a deep place of wanting to fit in with the stereotypes that the dominant culture believed about Latinos. Perhaps this came from what media presented to those outside of Latino descent as to what Latinos looked like, acted like, and sounded like. So whether that was having an accent like Nacho Libre or Antonio

Banderas or liking all the spicy food, which is most associated with Mexican heritage, when I had the opportunity to act more Latino, I felt I was letting friends down if I didn't oblige. On the other hand, among my own people I found myself going back and forth about which culture to emphasize. With Mexicans there were moments I opted to act more Dominican or more American because that's what was easier for me to fake knowledge of. And it was easier to lean into one of those cultures in order to avoid the comments that told me I wasn't "Mexican enough." The same would be true for my Dominican side as well. Not having full knowledge of either culture—the music, famous TV shows, and so on—put pressure on me to act in ways that excused me for being different without having me directly confront the fact I had gaps in my cultural understanding.

Here's something these experiences have taught me: falling into a caricature of your ethnicity or race can dim the beautifully nuanced person you truly are.

When culture tries to put you in a box, that's hard enough to deal with. But perhaps even harder is when you find yourself making a box of your own and hopping right in.

So what do we do when we find ourselves becoming a caricature? How do we turn it around?

Master of Disguise

Perhaps you've heard the term *code-switching* in conversations on race and ethnicity. Sociologists coined this term, defining it as "the use of one dialect, register, accent, or language variety over another, depending on social or cultural context, to project a specific identity."[1]

I have to admit, I relate to this: I have a "white" voice, which is my more "professional" tone, and I have my "urban" voice when I'm talking with people in an urban setting. The toxicity in that sentence is fairly obvious. And the fact that accents are ascribed to a color or socioeconomic status is what I think of as "problematic code-switching."

Code-switching can happen in other ways too. Maybe you "perform" as the person others have always assumed you are— the tough guy, the sweet girl, the soft-spoken friend, or the life of the party. It's like when Hollywood typecasts an actor, giving them only roles that emphasize their looks, like the chubby guy or hot girl, or roles that are similar to their previous successes.

Sometimes it can take only one occurrence of your behaving a certain way for people to assume you're one thing. Other times, if you've been misidentified or shamed for your accent or vocabulary, you may suppress a type of speech in favor of a more widely acceptable way of speaking.

Not long ago a fellow Latino called me a "white guy" publicly because I used big words he said he needed a dictionary for. (We'd been discussing philosophy and religion, and I was using terminology I'd learned from my master's studies that I thought would help us work through our thoughts. I figured it'd help us have a more productive conversation.) To have one of my people call me "white" was a shock, especially since I am darker than most Latinos. After all the work I've put into becoming educated and the sacrifices my immigrant parents made to give me educational opportunities, it felt like a slap in the face.

Now, if I had changed my way of speaking to accommodate my fellow Latino's expectations, would I have avoided this insult? Yes. Would it have been an instance of problematic code-switching? Yes, again.

There is a healthier term for those times we use particular accents or vocabulary with friends and strangers. The concept is called the "Chameleon Effect." That happens when:

We mimic accents in order to assimilate ourselves with others and create empathy. We unintentionally mirror others when interacting by copying the other person's gestures, body language, tone of voice and accent, in order to bond with others and feel safe in social interactions. . . . There is even a part of the brain dedicated to copying this behaviour.[2]

In this sense adjusting our behavior isn't about disguising who we really are; it's about using a tool built into our brains to project empathy. This is not to say fake an accent you've just come into contact with or even a foreign or urban accent you have no association with, but rather, notice how your cadence and tone may shift when talking with someone of a different culture than your own, both domestic or foreign.

Context is also key to the way we speak. My vocabulary, tone, and cadence will be different in a job interview than it is with my homies. You might think, *Then you ain't a real one.* My response would be, if your identity is found in your accent or vocabulary, then you're not being your authentic self.

The way you speak to others reflects your level of empathy and social awareness. A "real one" cares about how they communicate in professional settings and with people who speak differently than they do. We are meant to sharpen our individual characters, not prove that we're Latino, Black, Asian, or white "enough"—whatever that even means.

The Myth About Double Dutch

We're all complex, but sometimes certain factors, like race and ethnic mixtures, are more pronounced. The battle to be wholly oneself is won from within. That's what this whole book is about. There is a myth we've all believed—that we have to choose which parts of us are acceptable or usable by God in our day-to-day lives. I am not talking about character flaws or our propensity to sin but rather the things that make us unique.

It's a little like the game double Dutch we played in middle school PE class. You remember how to double Dutch, right? It's when two people stand across from each other holding two long jump ropes, one in each hand. Then they start swinging the ropes in a circular motion, one at a time, so that someone can jump in the middle and hop over the two ropes in a steady rhythm.

Oftentimes this is how we believe culture works. There are two sides of a conversation or ideology, and we are forced to jump at the rhythm of the conversation, trying our best to hop over each polarized side without falling on our faces. However, in Christ there is no "their" side. Whether left or right, "right" or "wrong," there isn't a side that humans can create that is worth conforming to. Paul exhorted believers this way: "Do not conform to the pattern of this world, but be transformed by the renewing of your mind. Then you will be able to test and approve what God's will is—his good, pleasing and perfect will" (Romans 12:2).

We're not called to "jump" to the pace and rhythm of culture, nor are we supposed to be subject to the merciless swinging of broken people in broken systems. We're called to a different way of thinking about ourselves. With the mind of Christ, we are given access to God's will and perfect design for our lives. It's not about what *they* think is right or what *we* believe is right—not anymore, anyway.

Joshua faced this as he prepared to confront Jericho, a mighty city with a great wall, in Joshua 5:13–15. Alone near Jericho he encountered a being who we find out is the commander of the army of the Lord. Joshua, shocked by this appearance, asked the commander if he was with Joshua and is people or with the enemy. The response rocked Joshua and still rocks me to this day: "Neither" (v. 14).

God isn't interested in an us-versus-them type of categorization. God is looking to see if we will choose *him*. While culture is trying to push the pace and force us to play the game and jump the rope, God is inviting us to step away from the rules of a faulty system and choose him. Only then can we be conformed into the character of Christ instead of a toxic caricature molded by human ideals.

Putting Yourself in the Box

Now that we've just revisited my middle school years playing double Dutch, let's step back again, shall we?

Aah, the glorious fertile ground of insecurity and puberty. Do you remember your first day walking into the cafeteria during lunchtime? It might be in the top five moments of fear and anxiety for every person who has had to brave it. I remember as clear as day walking into the lunchroom at Garner Middle School, surrounded by the scent of body odor combined with AXE body spray, voice-cracking conversations spoken loudly from every direction, the swirling of hormones, and attempts to insert cuss words in every part of a sentence even if it made no sense. All of this would have been enough of a shock, but the biggest paradigm shift for me was a collision of my two worlds.

I've shared that I attended an elementary school that was more than 90 percent white, lived in a fairly affluent neighborhood, and experienced typical suburban life. I'd also spent four days a week with friends from our inner-city, Spanish-speaking, immigrant church on the Southside of San Antonio. Garner Middle School sat right outside my suburban neighborhood, straddling the Eastside of San Antonio, yet the school was surrounded by low-income apartments where many students lived. So when I walked into that lunchroom, I felt like I was looking at the totality of my social life, a visual representation of all my worlds in one place.

The question then became, who would I allow myself to be? That would inform the choices I would make, like who I'd associate with or how well I'd choose to do in school. Group-limiting thoughts guided me. Instead of feeling the freedom to be myself, a combination of the experiences and environments I'd come across until this point, I limited myself to one group. I ended up choosing the one I identified with racially.

As I shared earlier, my attire started to change. My speech started to change. What I liked started to be molded by my friends, like musical taste and sports. Before I knew it, the fifth-grader who'd walked into the school with a neutral style of clothes and speech warped into the extreme side of urban culture. This isn't necessarily a bad thing; it was just a swing for me.

It was like I put myself in a box and put a lid on it. I became limited in my relationships. I no longer tried to do well in school. I cut myself off from certain groups of people and even refused to wear my pants at my waist. (Today I think sagging was a terrible trend, but back then I was convinced it was the best thing to happen to fashion.) None of this reflected the values of the home I grew up in. In many ways, the hip-hop and urban culture I was adopting became my identity—not in the robust way in which the urban and hip-hop community was founded but in a shallow, anemic way that boasted aesthetic over authenticity.

Up until this point, I had selected a group to identify with—the Mexicans—but in a petty and juvenile way. The distinctions between the Mexicans and African Americans in the school had formed a type of tension that put me at another crossroads. Throughout the years my Mexican friends had sometimes called me "Black boy" and even "Indian" (from India) because of my skin color. I had resented them for it but kept hanging out with them, just to remain part of a group.

While I didn't share completely in the African American identity, I thought I might be able to find more common ground with them, so I spent that year with them, partaking in their culture. I didn't make a clean cut away from my Mexican social community, but I felt more embraced among my Black friends. Though there were positive aspects to these newer friends, I could sense the lid I had placed on my life in order to appease them. To keep up that caricature, I was constantly comparing myself to others.

Comparison: Looking Through a Black Mirror

I'm a huge fan of the show *Black Mirror*. It takes a hard look at human nature and societal issues and critiques technological advances related to interconnectivity. IMDb's series description reads, "An anthology series exploring a twisted, high-tech multiverse where humanity's greatest innovations and darkest instincts collide."[3] Chilling, I know. If you watch almost any episode, you can attest to the production team accomplishing what they set out to do, as most of the scenarios feel like they could actually happen someday, maybe even over the next decade. That double meaning of a "mirror" is so crucial to understanding the effects of social media and the internet on the brain and on society.

Some "mirrors" we look at can skew our sense of self. Seeing highlights posted online that have garnered attention or success can cause us to adjust our own lives—all because of what an algorithm has learned to feed us. Those algorithms are created by companies who are seeking more of our time and attention so they can convert them into dollars.

The Social Dilemma, a documentary/docudrama featuring professionals who helped establish Facebook, Twitter, Google, and Instagram, examined how social media has shaped our behavior. Chamath Palihapitiya, who was an early senior executive at Facebook, lamented, "We curate our lives around this perceived sense of perfection because we get rewarded in these short-term signals: hearts, likes, thumbs-up. We conflate that with value, and we conflate it with truth."[4]

There are more than 266 million Facebook users in North America.[5] Now we have Instagram and TikTok to add to that number. Oh, and soon to come are the Metaverse, an immersive virtual world being created by Facebook, and Web3, a third iteration of the internet. Yes, that's right—we've been through three lives of the World Wide Web. Web1 was used for publishing and reading information. Think more in terms of googling things. Web2 is our current iteration that's more interactive with information. Think more social media, Yelp, Twitch, and other interactive platforms. Web3 is the decentralization and pure ownership in the digital domain. This means the public will become more and more proficient in creating a digital world for themselves that isn't confined to a large social media company or any other third-party source. Think things like the metaverse, blockchain, cryptocurrency, or DAO (decentralized autonomous organizations).

Whether or not you have a firm grasp on it, the internet just keeps on evolving. And as we stare into that mirror, we run the risk of unforeseen changes to ourselves. If we look to it for our worldviews, our perceptions of life and reality will constantly warp.

We are always developing something in our lives, whether it's beliefs, opinions, knowledge, or relationships. We will be shaped by whatever we focus on. The threat to humanity is that we often aren't careful about where we look.

The apostle James reminded believers that the "mirror" they should dwell on and model their lives after is the Word itself: "Do not merely listen to the word, and so deceive yourselves. Do what it says" (James 1:22). He also said that looking at the Word and not doing anything about it is like a man who looks in a mirror, and "after looking at himself, goes away and immediately forgets what he looks like" (v. 24). Our actions truly show which mirror we're looking at, and clearly, what you look at matters.

I like the way John stated the power of beholding Christ: "When Christ appears, we shall be like him, for we shall see him as he is. All who have this hope in him purify themselves, just as he is pure" (1 John 3:2–3). There is power in where you put your focus and how long you spend focusing there.

Comparison, human to human, kills joy. It can even kill people. I am not a social media abolitionist, but we need to step back and consider the emptiness of some of the things we derive our worth from. Social media is part of our lives, but it is *not* our actual lives. We must remember that distinction if we want to be grounded in Christ and the image he is creating in us.

There are fascinating (and scary) reports of how social media use influences the way we retrieve, store, and value knowledge—proving once again that we will be shaped by what we focus on.[6] Maybe we're anxious about our lives because we've compared ourselves to someone we've seen online, or we're depressed because we're allowing ourselves to be bombarded by negative news. Maybe we're becoming a reflection of the broken world and the broken lens people are projecting through their social media accounts.

Whenever we find ourselves in these kinds of mental and emotional states, we need to reset our focus and return to the wise direction of Romans 12:2: "Do not conform to the pattern of this world, but be transformed by the renewing of your mind. Then you will be able to test and approve what God's will is—his good, pleasing and perfect will."

Our relationship with social media can be like my middle school experiences—focusing in one direction so much that it puts a lid on our lives. We need to investigate any areas where we've let this happen. Maybe we placed some lids on ourselves years ago and still haven't taken them off—lids that were placed out of self-preservation from a comment made about us when we were young or an experience that negatively marked us and kept us from trying new things like making new relationships or going certain places. That's why it's crucial we don't allow what we perceive on our screens to dictate who we are becoming. Christ should always be the standard we look to. In beholding him we are conformed to his image, maturing in our faith.

The last thing we want to be is a fifty-year-old living by middle-school rules. Our self-imposed limits and caricatures are powered by our pride (we're proud of what we do, who we believe ourselves to be, who we associate with) or by our low self-esteem (feeling rejected on those three fronts). But just think for a moment: Who could we be if we took the lid off?

More often than not, I am less anxious when I turn off my phone or delete an app or two. So I've created boundaries for myself and sometimes take social media Sabbaths. You may want to unfollow, block, or curate your feed—but you still might struggle with comparison (just like the rest of us). You'll need to determine for yourself what it means to be intentional about limiting social media's influence on your mental and emotional state, or anything that causes you to compare yourself with others in an unhealthy way.

As we do this, we need to consider how much time we're directing our focus externally versus internally. We have the opportunity to make what we focus on lead us toward

Christlike transformation. We can either prioritize that or passively allow an algorithm to dictate our feelings and keep us from becoming who God intended us to be.

Self-Talk: The Voice of Judgment

Let me tell you about a show I've not been the biggest fan of: *The Voice*. Maybe I'm jaded after seeing so many reality TV shows about singing and finding the next big star, but I see *The Voice* as an illustration of what I call our "internal judgment meter."

On *The Voice*, contestants perform a song of their choice and aim to impress the judges, just like other shows. But here's the twist: the judges are in obnoxiously large chairs that look like a cross between medieval thrones and seating you'd find in Disney World's Tomorrowland. And, oh yeah, these thrones are turned around, facing away from the platform. The judges have a button they can push that'll turn their chair to face the contestant performing, but they do this only if they like the voice of the singer.

It is natural for human beings to judge themselves based on performance, and we tend to "keep score" of ourselves to gauge our worth. I believe that inside us there are different versions of us in conflict. They're trying to outperform one another in front of a judge—and it's not the Lord. It's our own self-judgment. It's as if the thoughts and scenarios that run through our heads about how we interacted with someone, or are planning to interact with someone, or want to be perceived publicly, are the "performances" on the stage. We stand in judgment. We compare ourselves. We determine the worth of ourselves and others. And as a result, we foster pride or low self-esteem.

As we've discussed, if you're not intentional about what influences your identity, you run the risk of allowing the randomness of a broken world to sit at the judgment seat of your life and dictate emotions, beliefs, attitudes, and behaviors. This is not to say you shouldn't have confidence in your ability to do things well or your potential to succeed at a high level, or that you have to live lowly and quietly. What I am saying is, the source you derive your worth from may be what you use to determine others' worth, which can limit your interest in engaging with them.

The roots of prejudice, racism, sexism, demonization, dehumanization, and the like begin from within. They can be cultivated by those around us through culture, ideologies, education, the arts, or familial and authoritative influences. This division grows as we legitimize the power that comes with tribalism, the itch of being accepted by others, and selfish gain. You may be thinking that these are outside-in issues (group-limiting), not inside-out (self-limiting). But what we receive externally can be cultivated internally—and over time, we can find ourselves dishing that dysfunction back into the world through our words and actions.

How did this happen? Why are we this way? We can find a clue back at the beginning, in the garden of Eden. Adam and Eve's sin opened us up to sin at birth: "Just as sin entered the world through one man, and death through sin, and in this way death came to all people, because all sinned" (Romans 5:12). This means that every single person was born in need of the Savior, of individual redemption. As Jesus said, "No one can see the kingdom of God unless they are born again" (John 3:3).

This is why it is impossible to fulfill our eternal purpose and walk in total freedom without the redemptive work of Christ in our lives. If we're going to understand the intricacies of our identity and how Christ can redeem and restructure it into a harmonious calling, we need to recognize that it's not about us getting better at our gifts, talents, skills, or even behavior. Our lives are like cracked vessels that cannot hold the water of healing, forgiveness, compassion, and eternal life. We need a complete overhaul from the inside if we don't want to remain bound to the brokenness of our sinful and fleshly limitations. This kind of transformation silences the critic, the self-judge, and opens us up to new possibilities.

Imposter Syndrome: Who's the Imposter?

There was an online game created in 2018 called *Among Us* that had a surge of popularity in 2020. The premise of the game is similar to the card games Mafia or Werewolf, where there's a hidden "imposter" killing people on the spaceship, and players have to guess who it is. *Among Us* became so popular because of its interactive components. No one knows who is committing the murders, and on the surface everyone looks the same. After each round, there is a time to vote on who the group thinks is the imposter, and the game goes on until either the group chooses the imposter correctly and flushes them into space, or the imposter wins by eliminating the crew.

Living in a polarized society can feel like a game of *Among Us*, where hard lines are drawn and you have to fit in on a certain side, even if you don't truly belong there. You can develop a fear of being found out as an imposter for not completely agreeing or wanting to engage with a side.

I remember having to go through a long, drawn-out discussion online with "friends" who I now believe cared for me only as much as I would agree with them. They were shocked at some of my beliefs and opinions about what was going on in the world. This was while I was pursuing the conversation about race and how it related to my desire to live like Christ, and other themes like sexuality and politics that were taking place in the sphere of public theology. I heard things like "You've changed" and "I can't believe you believe that." It was almost like Scooby-Doo and the gang chasing a bad guy in a "haunted" mansion, then finally catching him, taking off his mask and, with a gasp, shrieking, *"Mr. Jenkins?!"* I felt like people were attempting to "unmask" my true feelings about the world, except I wasn't trying to haunt any corner of culture or commit any type of crime in conversation. Still, it was like they wanted to peg me as an imposter and flush me into space.

The harsh words we encounter from friends, parents, authority figures, or strangers create a breeding ground for *imposter syndrome*. It's defined as "the persistent inability to believe that one's success is deserved or has been legitimately achieved as a result of one's own efforts or skills."[7] For many who struggle with imposter syndrome, they can feel like a fraud.

But this may go beyond feeling like you don't deserve the success that's come your way, or that you don't have the skills to do something. This is where the facts of who you are become a point of doubt and contention in your mind.

Maybe you *have* changed. Maybe you've moved away from the neighborhood you grew up in and got a degree or a career you never thought you would. Maybe your views on a number of issues have evolved. Maybe your faith has grown bigger and wider. Let me tell you: that is all okay. You're allowed to change your mind, and you're certainly allowed to grow, especially in your faith. But that kind of growth can feel a little threatening to the people who only knew you (or *thought* they knew you) as behaving or believing one way. And when they encounter you after you've changed and grown, it might feel shocking to hear how they feel about your growth. It can make you question who you are and whether you're who you're supposed to be.

I've gone through many stages of life since high school— higher education, a couple of careers, marriage, and fatherhood. It's a fact that I have a degree, a job, a wife, and children. Having imposter syndrome, however, would give me a sense of *pretending* to be educated, a professional, a husband, and a father. I'll admit, it is tough to align your feelings about yourself with the facts about who you are. Making the distinction between what you feel and who you are is important in identifying imposter syndrome and exposing it for what it is.

Imposter syndrome can strike when a big change happens in life. We might overthink things until we're convinced we don't deserve the opportunity before us, or we don't deserve to be perceived in a positive way. Then we can start beating ourselves up about being where we are in life, regardless of how we got there.

The truth is, we don't really deserve all the blessings in our lives because there's nothing we could ever do to earn them despite our best efforts. We will never be perfect. But God knows that, and he loves us anyway. We do not need to carry the burden of performance in order to earn the approval of God, others, and ourselves. Instead, we need to hand over all of who we are, what we do, and who we're connected with to Christ and allow him to guide our thoughts and live through us. Allowing him into these deep, personal parts of our being allows us to be shaped into his image.

Does this mean he's going to do my job for me, study for my exam, be my wife's earthly husband, or my children's earthly father? Obviously not. But there is a way of being that Christ invites us into, a life that involves a much lighter burden: "Come to me, all you who are weary and burdened, and I will give you rest. Take my yoke upon you and learn from me, for I am gentle and humble in heart, and you will find rest for your souls. For my yoke is easy and my burden is light" (Matthew 11:28–30). As we submit to Christ, we find a new authenticity in place of imposter syndrome and true character instead of caricature.

Now that we've looked at some of the complexities, pressures, and limitations we encounter in life and the confusion, tension, and aimlessness they can cause, it's time to look at the one who came to seek and save the lost. He has more in common with our earthly struggles with complexities than our Sunday morning sermons give him credit for.

Jesus.

He might be from a neighborhood just like yours.

PART 2

A MIXED SAVIOR, A MIXED CHURCH, A MIXED MISSION

6

STRAIGHT OUT
OF NAZARETH

The Forgotten Minority

A friend of mine with Mexican heritage told me about something that happened when she visited the state of Georgia for the first time. She hadn't traveled much outside of South Texas, so she had not visited any place where Latinos were not the majority. She entered a store and was immediately asked, "Where are you from?" She answered several different ways, but the woman who'd asked didn't understand her, so my friend eventually landed on, "I was born in Mexico." The woman quickly changed her friendly demeanor and abruptly walked away.

I wish I could tell you these kinds of interactions are rare, but they aren't. My friend had been blessed to grow up in a city with hundreds of thousands of other Latinos, but for those of us who have lived in places as a minority, this happens frequently.

I have dozens of friends who have crossed the US-Mexico border escaping poverty, violence, and all forms of tragedy to be in a place where hope could be restored and they can build a future for their children. I've heard countless stories from the immigrant community about the tensions, challenges, and pain of not choosing where they came from and where they grew up. Yet despite the courage and tenacity of these people, depending on who you say the word *Mexican* in front of in this country, you might be met with a sneer like my friend was.

Let me tell you another story of a friend of mine.

He was a man of mixed heritage, born in a lower class. He spent his early days as an immigrant in a foreign land before settling in the borderlands of his home country. At the time, he lived far from the epicenter of high society, in a lower-end ghetto with a reputation. His neighborhood was of a mixed bag of characters, where people spoke multiple languages, and immigrants and foreigners frequently interacted and crossed through.

This man was a blue-collar worker, working daily with his hands. He wasn't from a rich family, he didn't have any substantial financial backing, and he held no network

connections to higher trades or government. He was an outsider, living in the margins of society and culture, associated
with a city with a bad reputation, and he held political views
that seem complicated and counterproductive.

He made plans to head to a bigger city and start something there. He gathered young, hardworking, hardheaded
guys who would join his journey to dream bigger, see farther, and live greater. They started to talk like him and walk
like him. After a couple of years of working together, they
parted ways. The man handed the keys to his business to
these young men who had learned from him, entrusting
them with its future. With little education and formal training, they lived the rest of their lives walking in the footsteps
of their leader.

Does all this sound familiar?

This was the mixed-up making of a Messiah. An immigrant from heaven. Fully God, fully man. Jesus positioned
himself in a broken world with no hope or future, inhabited
by a tangled mess of a people. He grew up and lived life with
them, he taught and touched them, introducing them to a new
way to be human.

Jesus chose to be born into a humble situation in the
middle of nowhere, connecting heaven to a forgotten place in
the borderlands of Israel and the Greco-Roman world, to a forgotten people cast aside by their polished contemporaries in
Jerusalem. And he offered a message that would never leave
anyone forgotten again.

The Mixed-Up Making of a Messiah

Our Jesus was mixed.

He dealt with a mix of complex cultural issues and diverse pressures throughout his life. He came from a line of people who were a mixed bag. We don't have a Jesus who was raised in a vacuum, operating outside the cultural rules of his time, but a Jesus who immersed himself in a particular people group with a particular genealogy, accent, and neighborhood. He brought his eternal self into this distinct time and place and experienced an upbringing, just like every other human does.

It's so easy to dismiss people's upbringing after they're successful. We tend to assume the road they traveled was an easy one, a gold-plated, rose-lined, smoothly leveled road without the potholes and speed bumps we "normal" people encounter. We like to view Jesus as *the* example of living a successful life. But he was exposed to potholes and speed bumps just like we are. The writer of Hebrews put it into perspective for us:

> Therefore, since we have a great high priest who has ascended into heaven, Jesus the Son of God, let us hold firmly to the faith we profess. For we do not have a high priest who is unable to empathize with our weaknesses, but we have one who has been tempted in every way, just as we are—yet he did not sin. Let us then approach God's throne of grace with confidence, so that we may receive mercy and find grace to help us in our time of need. (4:14–16)

Christ was the conqueror of a real life, involving real challenges and real temptations. He felt pain, sorrow, anger, hunger, happiness, and contentment because he was 100 percent human while being 100 percent God. Some people wanted him to lean into the strength of his deity in certain moments, or elevate his humanity at other times. But he never forsook one or the other, holding both identities in both hands. He remained whole.

I've tried to figure out how to avoid diminishing any part of myself. I've aimed to be a perfect one-third Mexican, one-third Dominican, and one-third American in order to be "one full me." It's an impossible feat I'll never truly pull off. But thinking of Jesus living from both his human and divine natures helps me imagine a new path for myself, one where I allow myself to be my "one full me," my true mixed self. I dream of the moment I express everything I am—every intricate part of my identity—all at once, in a unique and authentic way. Looking at Jesus helps *me* remain whole.

Jesus Had a Mixed Lineage

When we're trying to understand the way Jesus entered the world, we have to look at it through the big-picture story of the Bible. We need to see Jesus in context to understand how he is inviting us to live out our own journeys on earth.

So where did he come from? Scripture tells us the Messiah was going to come from the offspring of Adam (Genesis 3:15), through the covenant made with Abraham (Genesis 12:3), and through the line of David (2 Samuel 7:12–16). Adam is known as the father of humanity, Abraham as the father of the Jews, and David as the royal line to the throne of the Jews. The books of Matthew and Luke both outline Jesus' redemptive connection to all people through their complex genealogies (Matthew 1:1–17; Luke 3:23–38). Though *complex* might even be an understatement for these passages.

Think of all that happened in history between Adam, Abraham, David, and then Jesus. If you're like me, then you would have expected Jesus, who's descended from the patriarch of Israel and the greatest king Israel ever had, to have an entirely stacked genealogy featuring only the "who's who" and shining stars of the Jewish world. But that's not the case. Even though Jesus was on a redemption mission commissioned by heaven, his lineage had a slew of fallen leaders and marginalized women.

In terms of ethnic background, Matthew's account of Jesus' lineage identifies four Gentiles: Tamar (a Canaanite), Rahab (also a Canaanite), Ruth (a Moabite), and Bathsheba (who is believed to have been a Hittite since she was married to Uriah before David). This is significant because the Jews of Jesus' time elevated pure-blooded Jews. Matthew didn't have to mention them by name—Luke definitely didn't—but Matthew's primary audience was the Jews, so he was making a point. Perhaps Matthew was mindful that even the greatest Hebrew leaders were either married to Gentiles—such as Moses, who married a Cushite woman—or were mixed with Gentile blood—like Boaz, who had a Canaanite mother.

Nonetheless, upon Jesus' birth, his lineage was ethnically mixed. I think Matthew was hoping that, for the Jews, this would highlight that Jesus was not only the King of the Jews but the King of all people.

Writing to a predominantly Gentile audience, Luke took Jesus' lineage all the way back to Adam, making it clear that the plan of redemption through Christ was linked to all people. Before the birth of Christ, the plan was already in place: humanity's Savior would not only have an unorthodox lineage as a Jew but also be the offspring of Adam and Eve. This was prophesied in Genesis 3:

> And I will put enmity between you and the woman, and between your offspring and hers; he will crush your head, and you will strike his heel. (v. 15)

We often overlook the many names of genealogy when reading through the Bible. But when we start to understand the historical and cultural contexts they contain along with the overarching story of Scripture, those names reveal a profound insight: who we come from should never be considered a limitation or a source of shame. Jesus' family tree included both the nobodies and somebodies, and, through the life he lived, he redeemed their stories and their names, despite all their ups and downs.

Jesus Was Born in a Mixed-Up Environment, in Mixed Company

Moving beyond Jesus' lineage, his birth was a scandal, not to mention a little chaotic. Social pressures almost caused Joseph to break off his engagement with Mary—it literally took an angel of the Lord speaking in a dream to convince Joseph to carry out the unusual arrangement (Matthew 1:18–25). Then, Joseph and Mary were forced to go to Joseph's ancestral city, Bethlehem, for the Roman census. But when they reached Bethlehem, Mary went into labor. They couldn't find anywhere to have their baby, so the Savior was born in a manger with humble surroundings (Luke 2). And soon after Jesus' birth, the family was informed by *another* angel to flee to Egypt to avoid a massacre of children by Herod's decree (Matthew 2:13–15). Talk about an unstable entrance into the world.

The King of the Jews has a lineage "marred" by Gentiles and controversy, a birth story full of drama of the highest order, and all this before he even landed in what would be considered his hometown of Nazareth in lower Galilee—also known as "the hood of hoods" (as I call it) to the common Jew of the time.

Let's take a step back for a second. Jesus was born at the height of the Roman Empire. Our Savior walked into a time of geopolitical tension, religious corruption, moral ambiguity, systemic racism, institutionalized sexism, rampant sexual immorality, socioeconomic abuse, and unusually sophisticated means of incarceration and death. So basically nothing like the times we're living in, right? (Sarcasm intended!)

Remember the concept of a king without borders? There has always been a need for a king who exemplifies the pinnacle of victory over the darkness in our world. Maybe what makes the best king isn't someone who has ruled the largest empires or had the greatest cultural influence in the world today. We might be tempted to revere a ruler who has conquered the farthest lands or has had the most success, but what about an infinite and eternal kingdom with the goal to reach everyone, everywhere, throughout all time? What about a ruler who moves with that kingdom? If there's a recipe for success, perhaps the Creator of all things should be the best place to start. Let's look at Christ's example of a new humanity ushering in a new way to rule on earth.

Turf War

We've talked a lot about tension, both internal and external. Tensions between who we truly are, who we want to be, who others want us to be, and who society wants us to be. It's as if these rival gangs of beliefs continue to circle the blocks of the mind and heart, mounting up their forces and waiting to attack, causing us to question our identities.

How do we begin to reconcile these warring forces attempting to take our lives? How can we find peace during internal conflict when both outside influences and inside voices are in constant opposition? Does the life of Christ provide a road map for us? Can he show us how to best live a life filled with nuance and steer us through all its tensions?

In short, does Jesus get you? Does his life reflect the battles you face in your own life today?

I believe so.

Whatever challenges you've faced, know that you're not alone in the struggle, confusion, pain, or loneliness. We can find comfort and strength in our identity in Christ.

Christ's desire is to occupy the space of our hearts. His life, death, and resurrection were battle points along the way to winning the war for our souls, giving opportunity for us to have the victorious advantage and our identity anchored in him.

> If anyone is in Christ, the new creation has come: The old has gone, the new is here! (2 Corinthians 5:17)

> Behold, I stand at the door and knock. If anyone hears my voice and opens the door, I will come in to him and eat with him, and he with me. (Revelation 3:20 ESV)

> So that Christ may dwell in your hearts through faith. (Ephesians 3:17)

I hope to make this clear to you: God-led identity is an identity in Christ. If our identity is in him, then we share in his massive victory over the Enemy, the world, and the flesh. You can guess who doesn't like that: the Enemy. So we have to be aware that day and night, there will be battles that rage for our souls.

Identity is something to be claimed, whether by external forces (God or the Enemy taking over) or through internal conflict (us struggling and choosing). Someone or something is looking to lay claim to your identity, whether passively or intentionally. This turf warfare is vicious, and it's because the stakes are high.

The person who owns their identity can change the course of their life. Proverbs 4:23 says, "Guard your heart above all else, for it determines the course of your life" (NLT). Nineteenth-century pastor Charles Bridges wrote about this verse, "As Satan keeps special watch here, so must we keep special watch as well. If the citadel is taken, the whole town must surrender. If the heart is captured, the whole man—affections, desires, motives, pursuits—will be handed over."[1]

Throughout the year 2020, I struggled with the concept of my identity, finding my bearings on all these tensions within myself, among my family, and with society. I found that I didn't need a Sunday morning Jesus, or a prescriptive daily-devotional Jesus, and I definitely didn't need a highly politicized Jesus who seemed to be championing one side or the other. I needed a Jesus who was real. A Jesus who got me. A Jesus who could lead me.

I heard people brush over the Bible's descriptions of Jesus' mixed context, as if they weren't applicable to his experience or ours. I also heard people say Jesus understood where I was coming from. *Really, though? And how so?* Did he actually know from experience, or did he know because he knows everything, like a divine "Ask Jeeves" (old school Google, anyone)? Then one day it hit me: deep-dive studies of the context Jesus was raised in aren't exactly a mainstream focus. After taking a closer look myself, I figured it probably should be. Because there are tools for us in that part of Jesus' story.

So in this chapter, I am showing you a Jesus who didn't grow up in suburbia as part of an elite social group, or in the center of popular culture. I'm showing you a Jesus from the ghetto. A man from Nazareth. A rebel of society, culture, and religion who would ignite a revolution of the world with a backward style of leading. A teacher whose followers would cause such a great shift in their context that people would refer to them as those "who have turned the world upside down" (Acts 17:6 ESV).

Christ in Context

When we think of Jesus, we often see him through the lens of artwork, movies, and performances—though some of the portrayals of Jesus can be problematic, like the fictionalized portrayal of Jesus in the musical *Jesus Christ Superstar*, or the "white Jesus" paintings circulated throughout history. Even so, I believe there's merit in attempting to show a tangible Jesus.

The Chosen is a television series that gives one of my favorite portrayals of Jesus because of the artistic style and tangibility of seeing familiar stories painted in a new light. *The Passion of the Christ* is a brutal and sobering reminder of the realities of the cross.

I think, even as Christians, we see Jesus as an untouched Messiah who easily glides along his life's purpose. But we have to remember that the Gospels are very limited in the telling of their stories. I love how the apostle John put it at the end of his gospel: "Jesus also did many other things. If they were all written down, I suppose the whole world could not contain the books that would be written" (21:25 NLT).

Though this verse is hyperbolic, the fact remains that we know very little about the first thirty years of Jesus' life. We know his birth story, a brief intermission of the Egyptian escape, and the moment in the temple when he was twelve. This could lead us to believe that Jesus didn't face much adversity until his crucifixion. We might place him almost in the category of a mythical being who was detached from the world.

But that's simply not true.

Jesus had a job. He had siblings. He got thirsty, and he got hungry. He paid taxes. And he lived in one of the hottest places on earth during one of the most complicated regional governmental structures of his day. He isn't just the red letters in the Bible; he was real and walked with real people through real issues of the day that, in many ways, outweigh our current challenges.

Jesus from the Block

Nazareth's reputation can be summed up in this famous interaction between the disciples Nathanael and Philip:

> Philip, like Andrew and Peter, was from the town of Bethsaida. Philip found Nathanael and told him, "We have found the one Moses wrote about in the Law, and about whom the prophets also wrote—Jesus of Nazareth, the son of Joseph." "Nazareth! Can anything good come from there?" Nathanael asked. "Come and see," said Philip. (John 1:44–46)

Environments can affect people, and sometimes it's simply the prejudice that comes with being from a place of ill repute. In Israel, Galilee was considered the borderlands, similar to San Antonio and many other cities near the border of the southern United States. Jews from Jerusalem didn't look too kindly on a town at the crossroads of the Greco-Roman world, because Galilee had a reputation for mixing in other nationalities and diluting the Jewish identity. In his book *Brown Church*, historian and immigration lawyer Dr. Robert Chao Romero discussed how Jesus didn't "belong" on either side of the border, and as a result, he "lived a doubly marginalized life."[2] It's honestly exactly how I've felt as someone who grew up in a borderland region.

Many people in Galilee intermarried with Gentiles, and as a result, many were bilingual and even trilingual.

Scholars believe Jesus may have spoken three languages. His primary language was surely Aramaic, an offshoot of Hebrew widely spoken after the Babylonian exile. Since scriptures of the day would have been written in traditional Hebrew, he probably knew that as well. And since the conquest of Alexander the Great three hundred years before, a large portion of the population in the Middle East spoke Greek—biblical texts point to instances, such as Jesus speaking with Pilate, that indicate he would have known the language. When speaking Aramaic, it's likely that Jesus carried a regional accent, making him sound different from those who lived in Jerusalem. We see a sign of this when Peter, a fellow Galilean, denied being a follower of Jesus when someone told him, "Surely you are one of them; your accent gives you away" (Matthew 26:73).

Then there was the political climate. The Jews were under Roman rule at the time, bound by laws that exploited them and by systemic structures that empowered local governments to take advantage of them—for example, tax collectors like Zacchaeus and regional kings like King Herod had a proclivity to use the people in their jurisdictions for their own selfish gains. The tangled web of political chaos ran from the highest points in Rome, where assassinations became a staple of Roman elites, to the local levels, where the regional rulers could use autonomous rights to gain wealth and power over citizens.

This political climate prompted the rise of three religious factions:

- Those who compromised with the powers that be (religious leaders like the Pharisees and Sadducees)
- Those who would withdraw from society all together (like the Essenes)
- Those who prepared their swords for war at all times (like the Zealots)

These groups caused rifts within the religious community. People had to accept these major categories (or religious boxes, if you will) with no other real alternatives to live out their faith, which ultimately led to huge distortions in the way people expressed their faith.

And what about Jesus' socioeconomic and religious background? He grew up in a working-class family, taking part in the family business of carpentry. This was not the work of educated individuals, but rather skill work; in some ways, carpenters were considered the handymen of the ancient world because of their ability to work with many types of materials on many different types of projects.[3] Customs of the time suggest that Jesus participated in his father's trade until the launch of his ministry in his thirtieth year. We also know Jesus visited synagogues in the area at a very young age; our Savior was raised in and shaped by that setting.

From this vantage point we can truly take a better look at our "mixed Messiah."

But he was going to deal with his mixed background the way no other human had ever done. Luke 2 discusses a key moment when Mary lost Jesus, just a twelve-year-old kid, after their time in Jerusalem during the annual Passover festival. After three excruciating days of searching, Mary and Joseph found him in the temple courts sitting among the religious teachers. The exchange between Jesus and his parents gives us some background on how our Savior would wade through interpersonal relationships and his calling on earth. To his concerned parents, he uttered a remarkable statement for a twelve-year-old: "Didn't you know I had to be in my Father's house?" (v. 49). Jesus was discussing the will of his heavenly Father while receiving direction from his earthly mother; it had to have made for an awkward moment. It led Jesus to obey Mary. And it led Mary, though in confusion, to cherish these moments before Jesus was to be launched into his full-time ministry on earth.

Both God and man, Jesus was about to show us something only he could: the way to be fully one's self in any context.

So this was the world Jesus was born into and the situation in which he started his ministry. As you can see, it was just as mixed-up and chaotic as the world we experience today. If we need a reason to be confident that Jesus knows what we're going through, we can find plenty of it here.

But let's continue. Now that we know about the "kingdom" he was born into, let's explore the "kingdom" he came to create through his ministry. You might be surprised to learn that it is also mixed in a beautiful way.

7

A NEW WAY TO BE HUMAN

Humanity Remixed

Jesus, like us, made his way through a fallen world. The issues of sin and brokenness existed then just as they do today. But he set out to change them. He showed us how to live in our mixed-up reality *and* deal with sin. The fall of humanity in the garden of Eden started the downward spiral of humanity and creation, and Jesus came to redeem it all.

The sin started with Adam. But it was about to meet its match in the "last Adam," Jesus Christ.

The Scriptures tell us, "The first man, Adam, became a living person." But the last Adam—that is, Christ—is a life-giving Spirit. . . . Adam, the first man, was made from the dust of the earth, while Christ, the second man, came from heaven. . . . Just as we are now like the earthly man, we will someday be like the heavenly man. (1 Corinthians 15:45, 47, 49 NLT)

Jesus was God's "plan A" for the redemption of the world. He became the bridge between God and humanity, operating as the sacrifice in our place. Once a relationship with God was possible through faith in him, God's presence could start to manifest in and among his people.

Christ's redeeming act ushered in the flourishing of humanity. Flourishing, or "the good life," is the central point of this redemption arc over the entire Bible. Theologian Jonathan Pennington put it this way:

Human flourishing is in fact a key biblical theme woven through the whole canon. . . . The Bible, across its whole Christian canon of both Old and New Testaments, is providing its own God-of-Israel-revealed-in-Jesus-Christ answer to the foundational human question of how to flourish and thrive.[1]

To me, this is a huge relief. It takes the pressure off and gives me permission to thrive, even in a complicated and confusing environment.

Jesus' purpose on earth was to carry out this redemption plan, marked out since the beginning of time. He clearly mentioned his purpose as he contrasted the Enemy's own intent for humanity: "The thief comes only to steal and kill and destroy; I have come that they may have life, and have it to the full" (John 10:10).

Does this mean everything will be easy after Christ has done his work in us? No. He doesn't wave a magic wand to create a comfortable life or an abundance of material possessions for us. But he definitely produces a life worth living.

Jesus' life reflects the tension of being in a broken world and also conquering it. After telling his disciples about the difficulties in their future, Jesus said, "I have told you these things, so that in me you may have peace. In this world you will have trouble. But take heart! I have overcome the world" (John 16:33).

Paul echoed this later in the New Testament, having seen it in action. It's the reality of the triumphant, all-powerful Jesus: "In Christ all the fullness of the Deity lives in bodily form, and in Christ you have been brought to fullness. He is the head over every power and authority" (Colossians 2:9–10). Not only is he triumphant, but he puts his power and life into his people.

You might be thinking, *Easy for Paul to say.* But remember, Paul endured relentless trials in service to Christ. And yet he was able to write these words *while in prison*:

Not that I was ever in need, for I have learned how to be content with whatever I have. I know how to live on almost

131

nothing or with everything. I have learned the secret of living in every situation, whether it is with a full stomach or empty, with plenty or little. For I can do everything through Christ, who gives me strength. (Philippians 4:11–13 NLT)

Yes, that's right. Your favorite gym verse, Philippians 4:13, was written about being content in prison and other grueling circumstances, because Christ gives us the strength for it. Perhaps you could stretch it to apply to bench pressing, but that's not nearly as challenging as persevering through the threat of torture and death for your faith.

So when we're grappling with all the dynamics of life—dealing with curveball after curveball, making mistakes we wish we hadn't made, enduring unjust treatment from others, or just experiencing the brokenness of this world—we can find relief in knowing that Jesus invites us to accept his life. The fullness of life. It's what he came to do.

Been There, Done That

I'm direction deficient. Meaning, if it weren't for Siri, I would be broke after wasting gas trying to get to the simplest of places. Or I would be divorced because of my stubborn inability to pull over and ask someone if I'm lost after an hour of fighting with my wife about which exit to take and whether we passed that Wendy's already. I am not the person you want to ask for directions.

Now, navigating cities with road systems, neighborhoods, and landmarks is one thing. Trying to navigate a life with past hurts, dynamic relationships, unpredictable political climates, and a slew of other things is nigh impossible—unless you have someone who has traveled the landscape, marked out a path, and brought a map and tools for you to use.

Jesus knew navigating this life would be hard for us, so he talked about how we could face the obstacles of our mixed-up world. He's been there. He's done that. And he knew what we'd be up against.

He Knew It Would Be Hard to Submit

Some of the most difficult words of Jesus are about how to follow him, especially this almost paradoxical description from Matthew 16: "Whoever wants to be my disciple must deny themselves and take up their cross and follow me. For whoever wants to save their life will lose it, but whoever loses their life for me will find it" (vv. 24–25).

The heaviness, and perhaps the beauty, of this command is that Jesus is inviting us to give ourselves to him—every part of our lives. This mirrors the way our Savior lived even *before* he picked up a physical cross: in full submission to the Father's will, no matter how big or small.

And this played out amid extreme trials. Jesus faced obstacle after obstacle, and he handled them with strength and wisdom. He defeated the devil on every temptation, and even in death. So remember that "we do not have a high priest who is unable to empathize with our weaknesses, but we have one who has been tempted in every way, just as we are—yet he did not sin" (Hebrews 4:15).

Jesus not only proved he understands our struggles, but he also blazed a trail for us. He now invites us to follow him with our own crosses, knowing that *he gets us*. And we can look to him for help, no matter the challenge in front of us.

He Knew We Would Be Tempted

Within the first moments of his ministry, Jesus was led out into the wilderness by the Holy Spirit to be tempted by the devil (Matthew 4:1). Yes, you heard that right—*led by the Holy Spirit to be tempted by the devil*. These temptations were specifically designed to test Jesus' own identity and validity as the Son of God, sent to earth for the purpose of redeeming humanity.

Scripture tells us that sin has three temptations at the root. We hear about them in 1 John 2:16: "Everything in the world—the lust of the flesh, the lust of the eyes, and the pride of life—comes not from the Father but from the world." Jesus battled these three desires during his time in the wilderness, and they're familiar to us too: things we desire with our flesh, with our pride, and with our eyes. Let's dig in.

1. Tempted by "the Flesh": When We Want More, Better, Faster

First, during those forty days in the desert, Jesus was fasting, so he surely experienced the "lust of the flesh," a temptation associated with the undeniable hunger he must have felt. "The tempter came to him and said, "If you are the Son of God, tell these stones to become bread" (Matthew 4:3).

Jesus' reply was based on the importance of prioritizing the spiritual self over temporary physical satisfaction: "It is written: 'Man shall not live on bread alone, but on every word that comes from the mouth of God'" (v. 4).

Here, Jesus showed us that we should make the Word more central to our existence than even the food that fuels our bodies. Jesus' denial of the flesh—prioritizing the nourishment of his spirit even after going weeks without food—should get us thinking of the things we think sustain us. What do we believe keeps us from burning out? As our flesh pulls us toward the poison-in-disguise the world offers to us, how can we prioritize the spirit's nourishment, like Jesus did?

Let's also consider the pace of our lives and the busyness that seems to consume us. We're driven by a type of hunger for *more, better, faster.* We're all starving for something. Some of us consume, consume, consume, trying to fill that hunger. Others work, work, work, trying to win approval and success by striving longer and harder than everyone else.

But more is not always better. Faster isn't always ideal. Harder is not always more effective. Perhaps burnout is derived from this hunger. Maybe our anxiety is birthed from a belief that if we try harder in our own strength, we'll matter more—to our families, to our bosses, even to strangers we don't know. But if that's what we're focused on, then we're missing one key thing: the life we live is a spiritual one. We don't need to be led by our insecurities to make things happen; we need to trust we can accomplish more *with* God than *for* God. Pursuing him and seeking his Word fills us more than those empty calories of *more, better, faster*.

I've heard people say, "Jesus never ran. He walked." Now, his ministry took place in just three years. That's a pretty short time to accomplish the redemption of humanity, so you'd think at some point he'd have to run. But no. His purpose and identity set his walking pace, like his detour through Samaria (John 4:4–42). His late night of prayer after sending out his disciples, only to catch up to them by walking on water (Mark 6:45–52). His tardiness to heal his friend Lazarus (John 11). Jesus' "leisurely" pace produced revelations of his power that broke down barriers of sexism, racism, and even death. His mission was redemption. His gain was his people. His home was heaven.

It's no surprise he said that "the Son of Man has no place to lay his head" (Matthew 8:20); his focus wasn't on building an earthly home. As a carpenter he certainly could have, but Jesus didn't allow short-term satisfaction to dictate his eternal mission.

If we don't have our identities grounded in eternity, then any temptation to satisfy a carnal desire will overtake us. In his epistle, James—the literal brother of Jesus—walked believers through the concept of a "desire of the flesh" and what happens when you fully act on that desire. James didn't mince words here. He said that evil desires give birth to sin and, once fully grown, sin gives birth to death (James 1:14–15).

When we deal with temptation of the flesh Jesus' way, it doesn't have to get to that point. Instead of *more, better, faster,* we can look for *less, simpler, slower.* We can take time to pause and remember our identity. It's hard to do, but Jesus showed us it's possible.

2. Tempted by "the Pride of Life": When We Crave Validation

Next, the Enemy took a shot directly at Jesus' relationship with the Father, saying essentially, "If you are the Son of God, jump off this tower and see if the angels catch you" (Matthew 4:6, author's paraphrase). He tempted Jesus to harm himself just to see the Father demonstrate his love and protection.

This temptation reflects something we all face in relationship to God—broken trust and the unhealthy need for tangible validation, instead of relying on faith in God's will.

The pride of life is isolating. It seeks to break off relationships and create division among people. It prioritizes self above all else. It's also often intermingled with insecurity, which can become a barrier in relationships. Through subtle or even drastic actions, we might push people to respond to us in certain ways in order to feel validated by them. It's a move that isn't restorative; it's just scratching a scab from a relational wound that will never heal until we give it the right treatment.

When Jesus came to redeem the world, he came to restore all our relationships with the Father. He was making a new family that would find a home with him, one with enough rooms and seats at the table for everyone (John 14:1–6). He came to connect us, but we can't connect to the new way of being family if we use an old system to relate with one another.

In order to be welcomed into this family, Jesus asked us to do the most counterintuitive thing: "If anyone comes to me and does not hate father and mother, wife and children, brothers and sisters—yes, even their own life—such a person cannot be my disciple" (Luke 14:26).

I bet I can guess what you're thinking. *Whoa, hold up. What does this mean?* Does this new family require us to forsake our old family? No, not really. What Jesus is saying here is that in order to embrace our divine ID, we need to release control over how we'd like to speak, who we interact with, and how we love others, even our biological families. We need to allow Christ to become the mediator between us and everyone in our lives. In order to embrace our place in our new family and our new way of living, we need to let go of seeking validation and seek the will of the Father with a pure heart, knowing our relationship with him is unbreakable.

There's a story in Matthew 12 where someone approached Jesus while he was ministering in a home and told him that Jesus' mother and brothers were outside wanting to speak with him. With no hesitation Jesus responded with "'Who is my mother, and who are my brothers?' Pointing to his disciples, he said, 'Here are my mother and my brothers. For whoever does the will of my Father in heaven is my brother and sister and mother'" (vv. 48–50).

This established a higher form of family, and we are led to assume Mary and her sons never spoke ill of Jesus for this. I don't believe he meant this as offensive. I believe he was calling us to a greater, all-encompassing relationship with God.

The complexity of our relationships is not foreign to Jesus' experience. Though he could've sought people's approval, or exploited any of his relationships for his own gain or expediency in his mission, Jesus remained faithful to his relationship with the Father above everything else. And with the love of the Father, he was able to offer salvation to those he loved.

We have to learn to avoid tangling our personal relationships with our connection to God, or allowing division and disunity to creep into our lives. The only way we can love one another properly is through experiencing God's matchless love for us.

3. Tempted by "the Eyes": When We Obsess Over Power

The last temptation, the lust of the eyes, came with the Enemy's offer to fulfill Jesus' purpose as the Messiah. For this last temptation, the devil took Jesus high on a mountain, overlooking what I bet was probably a beautiful vista, where the two of them could see the land and all its riches. And in that moment, the devil told Jesus that all he had to do to gain the nations of the earth was to bow down to the devil.

Jesus shot back a quick reply, offended at the mere thought of forfeiting the true path to atonement: "Away from me, Satan! For it is written: 'Worship the Lord your God, and serve him only'" (Matthew 4:10).

Though Jesus could've received the kingdoms of the earth,

he knew these kingdoms were nothing in comparison to the eternal kingdom he was about to establish. What the Enemy offered wasn't the real deal. Any kingdom he gave would be rife with injustice and exploitation, while Jesus' kingdom was all about restoring right relationships with creation, among all people, and with God. And it would be led by the greatest King. So Jesus rejected the option of expediency and refused to submit to the ruling patterns of this world, and as he did, he opened the door for a new kingdom with new rules.

Do you ever wish you were in charge of everything? That you could rule over your life and everyone in it with just a word? Change it all with a snap of your fingers? I hate to say it, but the grass isn't greener on the other side. There's no "there" that will ever fulfill what you were anointed to do and who you were anointed to be "here." This temptation to look around and wish you had what they have, or wait until you can get that, or jump ship to something else because what is being done over there looks better and easier than what you're trudging through here. This temptation to leave for the sake of gain in the moment can forfeit the fullness of what God has prepared for you.

There's no doubt about it: we'll face our own versions of this temptation. Maybe it'll be to cut corners in our work or to exploit people or situations to reach our goals. Maybe it will be to seek fame or take credit or make someone feel inferior to us, that they are weak and we are strong. But in a thousand little ways, we can respond more like Jesus, submitting to the Father God instead. Doing the completely unpredictable, humble, hard thing—the Jesus thing.

When we're tempted, we have the tools Jesus gave us. And they turn everything upside down.

Upside-Down Rules

Maybe you've heard that Jesus operated in an upside-down kingdom. Need some evidence? Just look at the way he contradicted how things usually worked: in Jesus' ministry, he championed ideas like "the first will be last" (Matthew 20:16), "the foolish things of the world [will] shame the wise" (1 Corinthians 1:27), and "[God's] power is made perfect in weakness" (2 Corinthians 12:9). So many things about Jesus' way were utterly surprising. And that's why his upside-down rules changed the world he lived in and continues to change ours.

Tempted by the Flesh? Love Your Enemies

When Jesus discussed enemies, he didn't discuss them in the way the rulers of his time did. Contrary to popular opinion (even to this day), he said to treat them with sacrificial love: "Love your enemies, do good to those who hate you, bless those who curse you, pray for those who mistreat you. . . . Lend to them without expecting to get anything back. . . . Be merciful, just as your Father is merciful" (Luke 6:27–28, 35–36).

For the people who were listening to Jesus speak, their enemies included not only the person they didn't like because of some petty disagreement. Their enemies also included the Romans and Samaritans—those who weren't considered the people of God. Jesus told his audience here to forgive those who had abused and harmed them. Talk about a radical way of living.

This is the same loving forgiveness we see in Jesus when he was on the cross. "Father, forgive them," he said, "for they do not know what they are doing" (Luke 23:34). When we're tempted by our flesh in the hunger for *more, better, faster,* and hungering for success, we are tempted to toss people aside or dismiss those who get in our way. We're tempted to cut off anyone who crosses us. But what if we stopped and forgave? That's what Jesus did, and it gave us a new outlook on achievement: the kind that lets humility and forgiveness lead.

Tempted by Pride? Lead as a Servant

During Jesus' crucifixion a sign that said "THE KING OF THE JEWS" was placed at the top of the cross (John 19:19). The Romans put it there as a gesture of mockery, and the Jewish religious leaders refuted it. The Jews, after all, had been expecting a Messiah who would deliver them from earthly empires, so they resented Jesus' claim of being the Messiah. He hadn't come on a white horse. He wasn't a military strategist. But Jesus knew who he was. He didn't need that kind of validation. He knew that the kingdoms of this world, though impressive to the eye, are but dust in comparison with eternity.

Jesus, the real King, could have given an order to take over the world from that cross. He'd said as much to Peter right before he was arrested: "Do you think I cannot call on my Father, and he will at once put at my disposal more than twelve legions of angels?" (Matthew 26:53). Peter had wanted to take matters into his own hands and not let Jesus be taken captive. He'd wanted to lead with pride and force (remember in John 18:10 when Peter cut off the ear of the high priest's servant?). But that was not Jesus' way.

Peter knew Jesus' identity. He had confessed, "You are the Messiah, the Son of the living God" (Matthew 16:16). Yet he rebuked Jesus for wanting to go through with his sacrifice on the cross. Jesus remained firm in his focus, committed to doing God's work in God's way. He would bring about change through humility, service, and sacrificial love.

The moment turned heated *real* quick. "Jesus turned and said to Peter, 'Get behind me, Satan! You are a stumbling block to me; you do not have in mind the concerns of God, but merely human concerns'" (Matthew 16:23). Sounds harsh, but Jesus was abundantly clear that he didn't need to be acquitted in the court of human opinion and spared the sentence; he had a higher mission.

Was it true that the Messiah was going to liberate God's people? Yes. But it would take some time for these Jewish disciples to get behind the real Messiah and his plans for a world takeover, because the concepts he was operating under were completely upside down. If Jesus didn't let pride get in the way during difficult situations, we can turn to him as we face ours. If he didn't lead by force, we can ask him to help us lead through service, even if it requires sacrifice. Because we know what it's like to look to a bigger plan.

Tempted by Power? Find Victory Through Death

Normally death means defeat. But for Jesus, it would mean ultimate victory.

Jesus wasn't going to be rushed. He wasn't going to take the easy way. He would redeem the world through the life he lived, the cross he endured, and the resurrection he had planned. This was the true power of the totality of his life.

Jesus lived with upside-down rules and resisted temptation. How? By relying on the power of the Spirit (Luke 4:1) and the Word of God. When we feel pulled toward the ways of the world or tempted by the desires of eyes, flesh, and pride, both the Spirit and the Word are available to us. As Paul said, "God is faithful; he will not let you be tempted beyond what you can bear. But when you are tempted, he will also provide a way out so that you can endure it" (1 Corinthians 10:13).

Jesus' life tackled every sin we could imagine at the root cause. Perhaps there are new forms of sin and tragedy in our technologies and culture, but they have all the same roots of sin. Jesus' birth, life, death, and resurrection established a new way to be human. So when we're facing temptations and sin, instead of overpowering them on our own, snapping our fingers, or longing for a greener pasture where we don't have to face what's going on, we find strength in the death and resurrection of Jesus. We die to our own power and lean on his. Upside down and revolutionary.

Perhaps your head is still spinning around all Jesus had to endure to give us a shot. Maybe you feel like you've tangled up your life and managed to make it a mess. You might even think you're too far gone to walk out God's calling. The truth is, you are. But Jesus isn't. Because of all he conquered, he has the keys to help you conquer as well.

This new way to be human is available to us every day. Every day you'll wake up with your flesh. Your need for validation. Your pride—and everyone else's, for that matter. Every day you'll wake up to temptation, but no matter the circumstance, Jesus has a way through. Your journey is not through the absence of trial or temptation, but it's a journey of having his authority in every situation.

So take heart and buckle up. Because after Jesus' ascension, a handoff took place. He launched his church into a lost world, using imperfect people. There was one individual who was assigned the toughest task and had the wildest conversion, yet he laid much of the foundation of our faith through his writings and example: Saul—the murderous Pharisee who was against the church—who became known as Paul, the faithful martyr for the kingdom. If anyone could show us that no one is too far gone, it is him.

8

OF JEWS AND GENTILES

Jesus Faith in Real Time

"Everybody has a plan until they get punched in the mouth."

Mike Tyson said this before going into a fight against the reigning heavyweight champion, Evander Holyfield. Years later, when he was asked by a reporter to expand on what he meant, he said, "[That quote's] application stretches far beyond boxing. It really has meaning in any area of life, whether the blow comes from a health issue, losing your job, making a bad investment, a traffic jam, whatever. It's how you react to that adversity that defines you, not the adversity itself."[1]

For Tyson, he'd entered that fight with Holyfield with a

plan, but through a series of strategic moves, Holyfield defeated him. Tyson lost in a TKO (technical knockout) in the eleventh round. He'd had a plan, and that wasn't it.

The same is true for the apostle Paul, who was originally the Pharisee and enemy of Christians known by the name Saul. He'd been on track to make gospel-spreading Christians pay with their lives. Big, bad plans. But he got knocked out along the way when Jesus called him to a whole new plan and mission.

We have our plans etched out in our minds too. They might look like a five-year plan, or a sales goal, or a target to reach a certain milestone by a certain age. Whatever the case may be, what do you do when your plans come to a halt, and, in a moment, you're faced with a greater purpose and a new identity in Christ? What will you do, and who will you be, when you get "punched in the mouth"?

When Paul was unexpectedly launched into Jesus' new plan and mission, he wore a few hats and titles that seemed to be contradictory on the surface. His name changed from his Hebrew name *Saul* to his Roman name *Paul*. He had the Jewish title of *Pharisee*, but he was also a Roman citizen. He was a Jewish leader who was called to serve the Gentile people. He moved from one world to the next, utilizing different aspects of his identity, as he served Jesus' purposes throughout his life. His complexities became his superpowers.

In Paul, we see how to live our new identity in real time, and we can look to his story when life seems to punch us in the mouth. It's believed that Mike Tyson's quote was based on the famous adage, "No plan survives first contact with the enemy."[2] And as believers, our goal is not only to engage the Enemy but to walk in victory over the Enemy in our daily lives. This is where the rubber meets the road.

Rubber, Meet Road

We often forget the Bible teaches us to live for Christ through relationships with complicated people and dynamic environments. Paul had a moment in the presence of God while he was on his way to fulfilling what he perceived to be his calling. But he was about to get rocked by the Rock of Ages.

In Acts 9:1 we see that Paul, who was then known as Saul, was "breathing out murderous threats against the Lord's disciples." A highly regarded religious leader, he was furiously making his way on horseback to Damascus to take anyone who professed this new form of Judaism, called "the Way," to prison and death. But Jesus knocked Saul off his high horse, literally, and began an encounter with him that would change his life.

> Suddenly a light from heaven flashed around him. He fell to the ground and heard a voice say to him, "Saul, Saul, why do you persecute me?" "Who are you, Lord?" Saul asked. "I am Jesus, whom you are persecuting," he replied. (vv. 3–5)

Saul had a plan—a religious and righteous plan, laced with passion and zeal for God. Getting knocked off his horse by

God wasn't it (he'd probably know how Mike Tyson felt). But plan or no plan, here was Jesus, and he was stunning in his power and glory. This origin story of Paul is so dramatic, it could be a superhero story in a comic book or movie. What an epic moment in the life of such a misguided and cruel man, and what an intense way to be converted!

Whenever we wrestle with our identity as Christ calls us, first we have to recognize that Jesus is the one who becomes Lord of our lives.

Maybe you've heard a preacher say, "Either Christ is Lord of all, or he's not Lord at all." In most contexts I've heard this statement, it's about surrendering your whole heart, whole life, and whole identity to Christ. It is something that Christians in the West have a hard time understanding because of how systematic church has become. Cultural Christianity is in full swing on Sundays, but all bets are off from Monday to Saturday. People want to live however they want and relegate Christ as King to just an hour and a half on Sunday. If we really want to engage with our God-led identity, we need to be ready to engage with the totality of who Christ is calling us to be, where he is calling us to go, and what he is calling us to do. No matter where we're traveling or what our plans are. Sometimes, like Saul, that takes a rude awakening and a total about-face.

As the story goes in Acts 9:8–9, 17–22, that encounter with Jesus physically blinded Saul for three days. Then a man named Ananias, sent by God, came and prayed for him. As a result, Saul's sight was restored, and he had a new vision: of

God's kingdom, fulfilling all he had strived to do in his previous life as a religious leader.

Scholars believe it took about three years for Paul's public ministry to develop within the region. Giving his whole life to Christ changed every aspect of his life's direction but still made use of all his strengths. In some ways Paul wasn't much different than he'd been as Saul, but he was now playing for a different team.

Switching Teams

Paul switched out his old jersey, one from a broken religious system, for a jersey of a different team—a new movement. He was mobilized by the greatest historical figure in history, Jesus. And he joined an already stacked movement full of Spirit-filled, hall-of-faith followers. He was a man who would be used by God to shape some of the greatest books in the Bible and spread the gospel to people farthest from God—a mixed population of outsiders the Jews believed to be the unclean, pagan, lost people of the world. These people were the Gentiles, or as the word is translated, "people who are not Jewish." In Old Testament times, Jews were to avoid speaking with Gentiles, touching them, or even *passing by* them. Jesus' trip to Samaria in John 4:4–42 was something the Jews avoided doing, which is what made it highly controversial.

Now, I'm a basketball fan, so Paul's dramatic switch reminds me of the time one of the greatest players in the world up and switched teams. I'm talking about the infamous trade of Kevin Durant from the Oklahoma City Thunder to the Golden State Warriors in 2016. If you're unfamiliar with this story, let me catch you up.

The NBA's Golden State Warriors had just broken the all-time record for the best regular season (which had been set by Michael Jordan's 1995–1996 Chicago Bulls, possibly the greatest team ever assembled in NBA history). The Warriors had been led by Steph Curry, who many believe to be the greatest shooter of all time, and an all-star cast of players, but they fell short of an NBA championship. Then they acquired Kevin Durant, one of the top three players in the NBA at the time and one of the best scorers in NBA history. Talk about stacking the deck against everyone else. One of the best teams in NBA history with the best shooter in NBA history, bringing on one of the best scorers in NBA history. This trade broke the internet and the NBA for the next several years. And it deflated my hopes of seeing anyone from any other team raise an NBA trophy!

So what does this have to do with Saul? Well, Saul's conversion did not take away his intellect, skill set, upbringing, zeal, or cultural complexity; it only honed it in a different direction. This is why the Kevin Durant trade lives in infamy to this day. Even though Kevin Durant changed jerseys, he was no ordinary player being traded. He was known for being the best scorer in the league, and many believe he may go down as the best scorer to have ever played in the NBA. At that level, the jersey doesn't dictate the play. Saul had all the things he needed to be a world changer. He'd been successful in his mission to stop the growing movement of "the Way" (a title for early Christianity), but ultimately Jesus' intervention directed all of Paul's skills toward helping it instead.

This was the movement led by Spirit-filled disciples, who had grown by three thousand people after only one sermon in Acts 2. If the devil was at a disadvantage before, then Paul joining the disciples was the nail in the coffin.

The initial launch of the church took place on the day of Pentecost (actually, in the sermon I just referred to in Acts 2). The disciples, along with 120 others, were filled with the Holy Spirit and able to speak in the tongues of the Jews who were present in Jerusalem at the time. This component of the calling was specific to the Jews and in particular those who were in Jerusalem.

Paul, however, was drafted by the Lord not only to speak in the synagogues and debate with the Jewish religious elites but also to take the gospel to the Gentiles. The outsiders. The mixed-up bunch that made up the rest of the world.

The church was expanding and multiplying, and when Paul joined them, they added one of the greatest thinkers and leaders of all time. He changed the history of the world as we know it—not because of who he was but because of who he gave himself to.

As we go deeper into his story, I want you to consider

all that has transpired in your own life. All the things that make you who you are. The strengths and weaknesses you perceive in yourself and the circumstances—unfortunate and fortunate—you've found yourself in. As we're about to see, Jesus can take strengths, weaknesses, relationships, upbringings, education, vocation, and so much more, and use them to fulfill the purpose he has for *your* life—in the specific way you've been designed. Yes, *you*. Jesus can and will take all that you are and redeem it for good. Not just for yourself but for a world he is looking to reach.

Paul's Greenhouse

Just as you and I weren't raised in a vacuum, neither were any of the people we read about in Scripture. So to appreciate this legend who shaped much of what we understand about our faith, and to learn from his journey, let's look at the soil he sprouted from: his geographical area, culture, language, education, and vocation. Basically, if he's got the seeds to a new church and a new kingdom, his background is like the perfect greenhouse for growing them. Maybe he didn't know it at the time, but it was all part of who God was making him to be.

Our first introduction to Paul in the Scriptures is when he was a young man of high standing in both the religious community and in the community at large, as a witness at the stoning of Stephen, the first martyr of the church (Acts 7:55–58). For information about his earlier years, we can find clues in other chapters of the book of Acts. He was a Jew from Tarsus in Cilicia (21:39), he was a Roman citizen (22:27), and he was a Pharisee and descended from Pharisees (23:6). Let's unpack that a bit.

First, his hometown: Tarsus. It was one of the largest cities in the region at that time, and it fell under Roman occupation around seventy years before Paul's birth. It was a port city, well established in trade and culture, and even boasted one of the greatest universities of its day, only rivaled by Athens.[3] Mixed population, to say the least.

Living in an epicenter of Greek culture and Roman rule, Paul remained deeply committed to his Jewish heritage as a devout follower of Judaism, like his father. His family, along with millions of others, were part of the Jewish diaspora that had put down roots outside of Palestine yet held fast to their religion, customs, and culture. So he had a family culture that was not native to the land he was in.

Several languages were spoken in Tarsus, including Greek, the common language of the Roman Empire, and Latin, the language of official documentation in the Roman Empire. People also spoke Aramaic, a language originating from the Aramaeans and adopted by the Jewish people who returned from Babylonian captivity. And there was Hebrew, the language that was used as the "holy tongue" to pray and read Scripture. All these languages were widely used and interwoven in the everyday lives of the citizens—including Paul. It'd be my guess that a guy this multilingual had to perform translation duties every once in a while.

All in all, it's safe to say that Paul was a mixed guy, and Tarsus was a mixed city.

Paul also held dual citizenship. During this time families of status or means were allowed to obtain citizenship of their city as well as Rome. We can assume that Paul's family was well established, given his father's position as a Pharisee and tentmaker, and that he inherited both of his citizenships from his father, as was the law of the time. Can you see why God had his eye on Paul for the mission he had in store? *Mixed* means *versatile*.

This type of upbringing would have turned a young man into a man of the world. His backyard was the gateway to so much diversity, education, and religious exposure, so it's no wonder that when we meet him in Acts 7, he is held high in status and leadership among the people: strategically brilliant and ready to engage furiously against Jesus' upstart church.

But here's the real question: What qualities from Paul's background could God transform into tools for his new mission as the apostle to the Gentiles? What were the things he had to throw away, and what was God redeeming for his purposes? As we're about to find out, nothing was wasted from Paul's early life experiences.

Wouldn't we all like to say the same thing someday? Imagine living a life and a calling where everything you've been through, everything you are, your mixed bag of experiences and attributes, all coalesce for the greater glory of God. A life where nothing—not the things you chose, not the things you didn't choose—is wasted. That beautiful vision is exactly what we're called to.

Waste Management

I'm not a habitual recycler, but I'll say that I am a recovering throw-it-in-the-trash addict. When I do recycle, whether at home or in public, I almost feel I need some type of recognition—probably because I got little prizes in elementary school when there was a competition to bring in cans to recycle. I'd dig through every trash can in our house for a week to collect those cans and even asked my parents to stop on the side of the road to grab beer cans left by the wayside. I was met with a sharp rebuke; the last thing my Pentecostal-church-pastor parents wanted was for their son to be seen walking into school with a bag full of empty Bud Light cans. But hey, if a pizza party was on the line, I was going to do the work.

Any type of recycling practice makes me think about other parts of my life I might like to change—to reuse and repurpose. I think of all I have gone through, everything I've done, everything I didn't get to choose for myself. What if I could trash all the bad memories, mistakes, pains, and physical features I don't like? I'd probably be tempted to do it.

Maybe you've been asked questions like, "If there's anything you could change about your past, what would it be?" or "If you could change any part of your appearance, what would it be?" We explore these questions in deep talks with friends and, in worse cases, as icebreakers in class orientations (although probably not the appearance one, thankfully). There's merit to wrestling through these thoughts and questions. Does God throw away everything after we give ourselves to him? Is there anything he redeems or "recycles" after we are completely dedicated to him?

As we look at Paul's story in Scripture, it's easy to see that all he experienced before and after his conversion was orchestrated by the Lord. But we can't forget that Paul was *living* the Bible. He wasn't aware of the grand scale of the mission to spread the kingdom or able to see how all his experiences would come together to help him complete his purpose.

Steve Jobs once said, "You can't connect the dots looking forward; you can only connect them looking backward. So you have to trust that the dots will somehow connect in your future."[4] Jobs never professed a life of faith publicly, though he grew up attending a Lutheran church with his parents. Still, this statement has a similar ring to a statement Paul made later in his life: "In all things God works for the good of those who love him, who have been called according to his purpose" (Romans 8:28).

Think about the redemptive nature of Mr. Miyagi's tasks in *The Karate Kid*. You remember *The Karate Kid*, right? "Wax on. Wax off." The wise old sensei trained young Daniel using common household chores. Day after day, week after week, the young man was pushed into accomplishing seemingly meaningless tasks that eventually turned into muscle memory he could use in his fights. Sometimes the tasks and experiences that may not seem connected to our training are needed for us to become effective.

Paul alluded to this kind of versatility for the sake of the gospel in his "all things to all people" exhortation.

> Though I am free and belong to no one, I have made myself a slave to everyone, to win as many as possible. To the Jews I became like a Jew, to win the Jews. To those under the law I became like one under the law (though I myself am not under the law), so as to win those under the law. To those not having the law I became like one not having the law (though I am not free from God's law but am under Christ's law), so as to win those not having the law. To the weak I became weak, to win the weak. I have become all things to all people so that by all possible means I might save some. I do all this for the sake of the gospel, that I may share in its blessings. (1 Corinthians 9:19–23)

Who knew that Paul would have all this backstory? And that, in the end, Christ would be able to use it to build the same church Paul thought he'd been equipped to tear down? Who knew Paul would use both his Jewish heritage and Roman citizenship to his advantage as he evangelized in various situations? It's likely he had philosophical knowledge from his upbringing in Tarsus and used it when speaking to those of different cultures. He also used his vocation of tent-making when evangelizing to the leaders of Corinth in Acts 18:1–4.

Called to the Gentiles as a Jew of Jews, Paul responded by

pouring out everything in his life for the sake of his mission. He used his complex upbringing and background as his superpower and didn't let up until the very end, when he finished his race in Rome. His last writing was about not having withheld anything: "I am already being poured out like a drink offering, and the time for my departure is near. I have fought the good fight, I have finished the race, I have kept the faith" (2 Timothy 4:6–7). His imagery of a life poured out as an offering depicts how God used all that Paul was for his divine glory.

So as we think about Paul, remember this: your complex upbringing and background just might be your superpower. And what I know for sure is, God has a way to use it that would leave you grateful for the life you've lived and the journey you're now on.

9

EL QUE INVITA, PAGA

Identity on Mission

Latinos often are subjected to awful stereotypes, but there are a couple I would proudly agree with. First, our food is flavorful (not just spicy—that's a Mexican thing more than a Latin American thing). And second, there's always going to be generous portions with enough left over to feed an army.

If no one is cooking and it's time to go out to eat, the common etiquette is the person who suggested the outing covers the cost of the meal. "Food's on me." There's a particular Spanish saying for it: *El que invita, paga*, which translates to, "Whoever gives the invitation has to pay the bill."

This is not only a Latino thing, of course. Parents buy their college kids' lunches, a businesswoman covers breakfast with a client, a boyfriend pays for his girlfriend's dinner. But in social situations where the expectations may be unclear, it's nice to have someone invite you out to eat and not have to deliberate over who's getting the check.

After his resurrection, Jesus gave his own grand invitation to his followers—a call to join him in his mission and step into their purpose: "All authority in heaven and on earth has been given to me," he said. "Therefore go and make disciples of all nations, baptizing them in the name of the Father and of the Son and of the Holy Spirit, and teaching them to obey everything I have commanded you. And surely I am with you always, to the very end of the age" (Matthew 28:18–20). To me, that last line—"Surely I am with you always"—is his reassurance that the one who has invited us on this mission will pick up the tab and provide.

This Great Commission is a sandwich of information that helps us understand what God is calling us to do. From the beginning, he has always had a redemption plan and a divine will for our lives. And remember, God can use the totality of who we are—anything and everything about our identities and experiences—for our good and his purpose.

First, the outside pieces (the bread!) of this Bible-verse sandwich: Jesus has all authority in heaven and on earth, and he is present with us until the very end of the age. Essentially we have a supernatural context that saturates both the front end and back end of this commission.

Then there's the meat of our responsibility: to make disciples, baptize them, and teach them to obey the commands.

This is a call to all the nations—which means moving out of our familiar settings as well as reaching people where they are.

In Acts 1:8 Jesus reiterated the Great Commission like this: "You will receive power when the Holy Spirit comes on you; and you will be my witnesses in Jerusalem, and in all Judea and Samaria, and to the ends of the earth." There is not an exclusion of the disciples' home bases, meaning Jerusalem. Nor did Jesus exclude the in-between places like Judea and Samaria. And the farthest reaches, "the ends of the earth," are not excluded because of distance.

If you were a Christian in the new church in Acts, you might have had several concerns. How would you deal with your family in Jerusalem or your crazy neighbors in Samaria? How exactly would you venture into the forbidden lands of the Gentiles, going beyond the borders of the known world and into vastly different cultures? The ends of the earth are a long, long way away, and who knows what you'll find there?

We'll each have our own version of these questions. And God will meet us and help us. We just can't forget that if we are to walk out our God-led identities, we'll need to walk where the Lord leads us and trust that he will not lead us astray. He's got us.

Favor and Suffering

Paul learned about God's faithfulness in some extreme situations. He was called to reach out to the Gentiles—to all the colors of the world, every tribe and culture, the frontiers of the unknown. Paul later recognized this honor and God's favor for him to be considered an apostle.

> I am the least of the apostles and do not even deserve to be
> called an apostle, because I persecuted the church of God.
> But by the grace of God I am what I am, and his grace to
> me was not without effect. No, I worked harder than all of
> them—yet not I, but the grace of God that was with me.
> (1 Corinthians 15:9–10)

He was the last person God called to be an apostle, but he had the biggest mission field, wrote most of the New Testament, and effectively changed history, all the while suffering from the systems and elements of this world.

> Five times I received from the Jews the forty lashes minus
> one. Three times I was beaten with rods, once I was pelted
> with stones, three times I was shipwrecked, I spent a night
> and a day in the open sea. (2 Corinthians 11:24–25)

Paul also suffered betrayals and dangers of all sorts while serving in his mission field.

> I have been constantly on the move. I have been in danger
> from rivers, in danger from bandits, in danger from my fel-
> low Jews, in danger from Gentiles; in danger in the city, in

danger in the country, in danger at sea; and in danger from false believers. (2 Corinthians 11:26)

This duality of favor and suffering is applicable not only to Paul but to all believers. Paul clearly articulated this in his letter to the Philippians while he was imprisoned.

To me, to live is Christ and to die is gain. If I am to go on living in the body, this will mean fruitful labor for me. Yet what shall I choose? I do not know! I am torn between the two: I desire to depart and be with Christ, which is better by far; but it is more necessary for you that I remain in the body. (Philippians 1:21–24)

I want to know Christ—yes, to know the power of his resurrection and participation in his sufferings, becoming like him in his death, and so, somehow, attaining to the resurrection from the dead. (3:10–11)

When we accept God's calling on our lives, we are not stepping onto a path of ease and comfort. And, truth be told, your life has probably given you plenty of upheaval and suffering as part of your background story. Moving into our calling, we can't expect full acceptance from others or constant effectiveness in our efforts. We need to be ready to deal with hardship like Paul did. Jesus' calling to us is full of favor, and our backgrounds give it flavor. But at the heart, our calling is to pick up our own cross daily as we pursue what he wants us to.

What does it mean to pick up our own cross? Basically, it's picking up our situations—where we are, what we're dealing with—and moving forward with them in obedience to Christ. For me, that meant picking up my story, my mixed background, and surrendering to God the things that bother and confuse me. This is part of the promise of the cross, oddly enough. When I carry my cross with Christ, I also get to carry his resurrection. I die to my flesh, which wants to project my mess onto others. Wherever I go, I allow that flesh to be crucified, and I get to live in the resurrection of my new identity in Christ! It's on display for everyone to see. My new identity becomes my testimony.

Holding favor and suffering with both hands isn't something we need to fear. For Paul, carrying the cross of his own calling led to the legendary story of a man who believed Jesus and chose to follow him to the very end. For you and me—who knows where it could lead? The one thing we can be sure of is that when we follow Jesus' invitation, we will see that he's woven our situations together for his glory.

Bigger Than "Missions"

San Antonio is sometimes called "the Mission City" because five Spanish missions were founded there—including the Alamo, one of the most famous missions in the US. San Antonio is also known as "Military City USA" because it has one of the largest concentrations of military bases in the United States. These cultural titles are significant because they reflect two lines of history intertwined as one. Missions were established by the Spanish to conquer native people, converting them to Christianity and establishing Spanish rule. Some would say this is not too different from how the might of the US military has caused our prominence in global affairs.

Today, much of the mission work done around the world no longer uses the unjust tactics of colonizing the "other" or trampling a foreign culture in order to spread the kingdom. In more and more cases, mission work has moved in the direction of advancing a kingdom and not a government. It emphasizes the restoration of people's dignity and helps them flourish through the redemptive work of the gospel, through the proclamation and demonstration of God's love.

Consider a common thread among Joseph, Esther, Daniel, Moses, Paul, and Jesus: they all were outsiders within a dominant culture, and they each became a bridge of salvation for the people they sought to save. *El que invita, paga.* If God gives the invitation, he'll pay the tab. As Christians we don't just navigate our ethnic or racial tensions; we also navigate our heavenly citizenship in an earthly reality. We're in this world but not of this world.

Even those of us who see ourselves as "in need" ought to be willing to reach out. We can trust that if he is the one calling us, we are not the ones having to "pay the bill" of strength, power, and resources. Taking the first step of obedience in the direction the Lord has asked you to go will lead to him providing what you need for the next step.

Dynamic Duo: Faith and Works

Trusting God to pick up the tab for us takes *faith*. We have to believe he will act through us despite our weaknesses. It also requires *work*—to acknowledge all of who we are and bring everything to the table for God to use. To make ourselves fully available to him and then follow through.

James wrote, "Faith by itself, if it is not accompanied by action, is dead" (James 2:17). And yet we see from Paul that our salvation is not anchored in what we do (work) but through our trust in the gift of salvation through Christ (faith).

> It is by grace you have been saved, through faith—and this
> is not from yourselves, it is the gift of God—not by works,
> so that no one can boast. For we are God's handiwork, cre-
> ated in Christ Jesus to do good works, which God prepared
> in advance for us to do. (Ephesians 2:8–10)

In other words, we need to be willing to obey and embrace who we are designed to be and what we are called to do, and trust God to fill in the blanks of our weaknesses and the lack of detailed instruction in his time.

No one in the Bible who accomplished anything for God did so with hard work alone or with idle faith. They all are proof that God's checks don't bounce. The writer of Hebrews wrote a famous chapter known as the "Hall of Faith" where he listed believers who, before the crucifixion and resurrection of Christ, had both faith and works as a part of their testimonies. Ambiguity and scarcity were a large part of these individuals' lives. The chapter begins with the baseline of faith: "Faith is confidence in what we hope for and assurance about what we do not see" (Hebrews 11:1).

Beautiful, right? There is no disconnect with these giants of faith in their obedience in action and their belief in God as they navigate opportunities placed in front of them. Though this list doesn't include every individual who believed God in the Old Testament, it does provide a common framework of how to live with faith in Christ. We may have little to nothing, or be seen as the "wrong person" for a task, or feel disqualified because of cultural norms—but we can still be used for God's glory.

We can see this in all sorts of people in Hebrews 11. Let's take a look at one person who didn't believe he was qualified. He had a pretty checkered past, but God still called him to free his people: Moses. And let's try to see him not as a Hall of Faith superstar but as a person in the out-group who received a destiny only God could have planned.

Moses: Prince of Egypt, Enemy of the State, Leader of the Exodus

You probably know the gist of Moses' story (and maybe saw the movie—who else loved *The Prince of Egypt*?). I want to pick it up at that famous moment when Moses had an encounter with God at a burning bush.

God called out to Moses from the burning bush by name. Moses' response was to answer the call by saying, "Here I am" (Exodus 3:4). As he began to draw close to the voice, he was quickly instructed to take off his sandals in reverence of the presence of God. God then introduced himself: "'I am the God of your father, the God of Abraham, the God of Isaac and the God of Jacob.' At this, Moses hid his face, because he was afraid to look at God" (vv. 5–6).

It's interesting that the interaction between God and Moses began with God's identification of Moses by name. Moses responded in the affirmative, and then God corrected Moses' posture and began to describe himself. I believe that if we're going to move toward the wholeness God wants us to walk in, we need to understand this moment. It can be broken down into a two-pronged interaction: God calling Moses by his name and God calling him by his identity.

God Called Moses by His Name

Now, you probably remember that Moses' backstory is complicated. Let's visit his backstory for some more details.

We learn in Exodus 2 that Moses was a Hebrew boy who escaped the Egyptian edict to eradicate all newborn Hebrew boys when his mother placed him in a basket and floated him down the Nile. After his miraculous escape by river, who found Moses? By God's divine orchestration, the princess of Egypt. As a result, he spent approximately forty years in Egyptian high culture, mingling with people from various people groups who would send their children to Egypt for education, learning customs, traditions, religion, and law. Knowing this helps us see Moses' encounter at the burning bush with the complexity of his identity and the context he was born into and molded by.

The book of Acts gives us a better view of his experience as a Hebrew boy raised as an Egyptian.

> [Moses] saw one of [the Israelites] being mistreated by an Egyptian, so he went to his defense and avenged him by killing the Egyptian. Moses thought that his own people would realize that God was using him to rescue them, but they did not. (7:24–25)

In his sense of connection to the Israelites, Moses reacted to the cruelty against one of them in an unthinking act of violence, an act of defense. Yet his own people did not recognize him as one of their own, much less as their deliverer.

> The next day Moses came upon two Israelites who were fighting. He tried to reconcile them. . . . But the man who was mistreating the other pushed Moses aside and said, "Who made you ruler and judge over us? Are you thinking

of killing me as you killed the Egyptian yesterday?" When Moses heard this, he fled to Midian, where he settled as a foreigner. (vv. 26–29)

Moses hit a moment when he had to choose between living as an Israelite or living as an Egyptian, and oddly enough he chose an alternate, even more complicated path—the path to Midian.

There's an aspect of this story that hits home for me, and it might for you too. You didn't choose your upbringing, your skin color, the language you speak, or where you attended school, yet God has put a passion in your heart that won't allow you to sit idle. And so you split at the dividing point of your various identifiers. (Granted, this is an extreme example involving murder. But generally speaking, I bet the passion and inner conflict here is relatable for most of us.)

If he wasn't confused already, Moses would be soon, because another variable was about to be added to the conflicting cultures within him.

Moses became a stranger in a strange land. He encountered some Midianite women who were being harassed, and he rescued them, but they were confused about who he was. When they went home, their father asked the women why they had returned so early from being with the flocks, and they answered, "An Egyptian rescued us from the shepherds. He even drew water for us and watered the flock" (Exodus 2:19).

Moses was an Egyptian now? Wasn't it enough that Moses was running away from the Egyptians because he'd murdered one of their own, while simultaneously being rejected by his biologically related Hebrew people? Now these Midianites identified him as Egyptian.

We don't know why they called him this. Perhaps all those under Egyptian rule carried this title outside of Egypt. Maybe it was the clothing he wore, or the language and accent he used during his confrontation with the shepherds. Whatever the case, Moses was starting off as an Egyptian in the Midianites' eyes even after losing everything to his passion for justice for his Hebrew people. Talk about a perfect storm for an identity crisis.

Nonetheless, he settled in the wilderness with the Midianite people, marrying a Midianite woman and having two mixed children with her. I think of my children when I read this.

Then we get to the burning bush. The man the Lord was looking for was a Hebrew runaway who had forfeited his adopted Egyptian pedigree and spent forty years as a Midianite shepherd. And the Lord called him by his name. Not his upbringing. Not his nationality. Not his criminal status. Not his vocation. Not even his membership to the children of Israel. "God called to him from within the bush, 'Moses! Moses!' And Moses said, 'Here I am'" (Exodus 3:4).

He was called *Moses* twice—that's it. No title, no nick-name, no criminal charge, nothing: simply *Moses*. This is good news for those of us who feel like we're spiraling in nuance and can't get ahold of anything solid to anchor our identity to: God has the ability to call you by the weight of your name.

Moses' name in Egypt carried the weight of criminal and fugitive. Moses' name among the Hebrews carried the weight of elitist sellout and murderous coward. Now, among the Midianites, it carried the weight of misidentified Egyptian, father, husband, and shepherd. Though we may assume that deep down Moses knew he was so much more, the weight of all these perceptions was probably a lot to carry—maybe even too much. He had been choosing to stay with the Midianites, raising a family, shepherding—a load just light enough to live with the rest of his days.

And yet, God said no.

All that Moses was, everything he experienced culturally, every action he'd committed, and every decision he'd ever made, was called out in one name: *Moses*.

God Reminds Moses of His Identity

Next up at the burning bush, the Lord told Moses to posture himself in reverence in God's presence: "'Do not come any closer,' God said. 'Take off your sandals, for the place where you are standing is holy ground'" (Exodus 3:5).

Then God introduced himself to Moses, presenting him with his own name, but not in any normal way. He said, "I am the God of your father, the God of Abraham, the God of Isaac and the God of Jacob" (v. 6).

The name he used for himself was attached to three other names of the fathers before Moses: Abraham, Isaac, and Jacob. The greatness of these men was felt among the entire Hebrew nation, but they were people with complicated pasts, journeys, and callings too. It was almost as if God was reminding Moses that though they had carried out the Hebrew promise and covenant, they also had complicated pasts. God had accepted those fathers' names, and now God was accepting Moses'.

We can see in this moment that the totality of who we are in name is the best way we can be addressed by the Lord.

Growing up in a Latino household, it was normal when you were in trouble to hear your full name with all the syllables enunciated emphatically. My mother never yelled my full name unless she was furious, scared for my safety, or had already called for me more than twice. There's something about being called by your full name by your Dominican mother that hits deeper than anything else. In that moment there is no confusion—you know you're wanted *now*—and there is also a sense of almost nakedness, like you're being seen and called out for who you are. It's even worse when you have siblings and your mother rattles off all the wrong names before getting to yours—it amplifies the anger.

In a serious way, God was calling Moses out—and not to throw a *chancla* at him. (A cross-cultural side note for you: The word *chancla* is Spanish for "sandal." It's famous for being the weapon of choice for any Latina mother, almost like Batman and his Batarangs. My mom had an impressive arm with a chancla.) Thankfully God chose words to confront Moses instead of a cosmically charged chancla.

In this encounter with God, Moses' journey of acquiring identifiers was over. It was time to find his identity and to learn what everything up until that point meant and what it could be used for.

The rest of the conversation at the burning bush was simple enough. God not only accepted Moses' name but did something even more powerful: he exchanged the weight of Moses' name for the weight of his own. In Exodus 3, after Moses came back with, "Who am I that I should go?" (v. 11) and "Who should I tell them sent me?" (v. 13, author's paraphrase), God said,

> "I AM WHO I AM. This is what you are to say to the Israelites: 'I AM has sent me to you.'" God also said to Moses, "Say to the Israelites, 'The LORD, the God of your fathers—the God of Abraham, the God of Isaac and the God of Jacob—has sent me to you.'
> "This is my name forever,
> the name you shall call me
> from generation to generation." (vv. 14–15)

Moses grappled with his cultural and ethnic identifiers, then he placed the burden of the complexity on God's shoulders. God took hold of it and gave Moses a name and calling that rose far above all the variables Moses had been considering. The Lord gave Moses God's own name. The name that God shall be called forever, from generation to generation. From the mouths of broken person to broken person. From one cultural context to another. I AM.

The cry of the people was for salvation. God's response was WHO HE WAS.

The I AM goes beyond cultural, ethnic, or historical baggage. He IS who he IS. That opens the door for anyone anywhere to be saved by him and be used by him. Because our identity is in him.

There came a moment at the burning bush when God directed Moses' attention to what was in his hand. Once again, here was a shepherd being called to so much more.

Moses had expressed his self-doubt to God, questioning how he'd possibly persuade Pharaoh to release God's people. "What if they do not believe me or listen to me and say, 'The LORD did not appear to you'?" Moses had asked (Exodus 4:1).

God responded with a question: "What is that in your hand?"

"A staff," Moses answered (v. 2).

Little did he know that one day he would use that same staff to lead the children of Israel across the Red Sea into freedom.

Let's fast-forward to that moment of crisis. At the coast of the Red Sea, with a speeding army behind them and the crashing waves before them, Moses cried out to the Lord for help.

"Why are you crying out to me?" God said. "Tell the Israelites to move on. Raise your staff and stretch out your hand over the sea to divide the water so that the Israelites can go through the sea on dry ground" (Exodus 14:15–16).

All you have is all you need.

Beyond all the other uses of the staff, this is a full-circle moment of God's provisional power emanating out of something Moses already possessed. It's a reminder that faith and obedience work hand in hand, making the impossible possible.

The writer of Hebrews gave us further insight into Moses' faith and works:

> By faith he left Egypt, not fearing the king's anger; he persevered because he saw him who is invisible. By faith he kept the Passover and the application of blood, so that the destroyer of the firstborn would not touch the firstborn of Israel.
>
> By faith the people passed through the Red Sea as on dry land; but when the Egyptians tried to do so, they were drowned. (Hebrews 11:27–29)

That's what God did with the little Moses already had.

Do you feel like you don't have what it takes to do God's work? That your background is too confusing, or you're confused about how to move forward? Perhaps he wants you to use what's already in your hands and to move "by faith." Perhaps he wants to invite you through your own version of the burning bush and call you by name.

Rest assured, he knows your name. He knows your story. And he knows what you have in your hand. The invitation to follow him still stands. The invitation to bring his love to the world still stands. The invitation to be used by him still stands—and is tailored specifically to you.

Do you have what it takes to do it on your own? Not really—and that's fine. It's part of the plan. You know that through the blood of Christ, *El que invita, paga.* He who has invited will pay the whole way.

EPILOGUE

I do a lot of running in my neighborhood these days. I picked up running during the Ahmaud Arbery remembrance, and I never stopped. I've moved two times since then—from Texas to Florida, and from Florida to Louisiana. I've had a steady diet of running in every neighborhood I've been in. Not for any deep reason, and truthfully not in remembrance of anyone or anything, only because I've developed a taste for the benefits of running consistently.

The health benefit, the mental factor, the emotional dumping—you could say running has now become a form of therapy for me. A reset every morning. The pace and length of my runs has evolved. I'm faster now. I can go farther now. I know my breathing, heart rate, and body better now. I hope to never stop. It is amazing what you can learn by just staying in it—by waking up and doing it regardless of how you feel.

This is a bit like how the journey of conversations around race, ethnicity, and identity have been for me. When I keep sticking with it, I keep growing.

A couple of years have passed since I began writing this book, and a lot has changed in my life. The world has changed. Conversations have evolved yet again. Many people have gravitated toward two ends of the spectrum: dropping the conversation all together, as if it were a trend that has now gone out of style, or adopting it as their entire mission and identity, not allowing anything in life to be devoid of racial and ethnic edge, as if the sum of our beings is founded on our historical realities and physical appearances.

I confess that I've run up and down this spectrum of extremes since the beginning of this journey. At times I've been so consumed by who I believed myself to be based on my physical appearance and upbringing that nothing mattered more. I've received countless invitations, from Christian stadium events to smaller, more intellectual settings, to either represent my community or speak from my community's perspective. There have also been months more recently when I have wanted to drop the conversation altogether.

The exhaustion of running from one extreme to another has been draining. Running, running, running, and feeling like I'm getting nowhere. Before one conversation about identity can find closure, the zeitgeist shifts with another definition of what it truly means to be human, and unfortunately our Western church has taken the bait and run to social media or their pulpits with more "hot takes" than foundational teaching around true God-led identity.

I constantly need the reminder that my source of self stems from the Creator himself. That conversations about our distinctions and wrestling through what it means to be human aren't something new, and they won't go away. Rather, I have to continue working to keep Christ at the center. In our culture, where the individual has been given so much autonomy to decide what is right in their own eyes, community has started to suffer. Amplify this with a globalized world, and now it seems incredibly difficult for people to relate to one another in a humble, generous, and integrated way. Unity has been harder than ever to attain, and I am seeing fractures in our churches as people have decided to go their own ways. Some leaders have decided to draw hard, black-and-white lines about who people should be, and others have diluted messaging down, trying to keep everyone happy and satisfied in their seats.

The truth is, if we keep evaluating our own self-discovery by external means, we will never truly find what our hearts are longing for. There must be a supernatural edge, a sword that can cut through the junk of culture and reach the places in need of the most change. Despite our steep decline in biblical literacy, we must understand that the voice of God is clearest through his Word.

Before his execution in Rome, Paul wrote to his protégé Timothy about the power and function of Scripture. Read what are essentially the words of a dead man who was full of clarity and conviction:

> All Scripture is inspired by God and is useful to teach us what is true and to make us realize what is wrong in our lives. It corrects us when we are wrong and teaches us to do what is right. God uses it to prepare and equip his people to do every good work. (2 Timothy 3:16–17 NLT)

Similarly, the writer of the book of Hebrews described Scripture's role in our lives as critical:

> The word of God is alive and active. Sharper than any double-edged sword, it penetrates even to dividing soul and spirit, joints and marrow; it judges the thoughts and attitudes of the heart. (4:12)

The Bible is the ultimate book of answers for our world today, a gateway to truth. Without the anchor of the Word of God, the revelation given by the Spirit, and an understanding of the example Christ left us to live with redemptive power, we are better off sitting down and keeping quiet.

I don't know about you, but I want to make my running count. I want to be able to echo Paul and say, "I run with purpose in every step" (1 Corinthians 9:26 NLT) and declare that I have "finished the race" (2 Timothy 4:7).

Maybe you've had moments of clarity while reading this book, or moments when even a revelation of right direction was given to you. You might feel ready to move forward on this journey toward inner peace amid external pressure. Wherever you find yourself now, I want to encourage you with this reality: freedom is not the absence of problems; it's the presence of Jesus.

He is the only way we can walk this journey. He is the leader. Sometimes it feels like he's leading us into the fire of controversy when our definitions of being human don't match the definitions of culture, but be encouraged that wherever he leads, he will be there—and if it's into the fire, know that you won't get burned!

Three young men in the book of Daniel faced a fiery furnace because of their steadfast loyalty to who they were as followers of God. They found themselves in the fire, and just as tragedy seemed to befall them, God revealed himself—not only to the young men but to the king and his servants, which would impact the whole nation (3:19–30). It was only in the fire that the manifest presence of God showed up.

It wasn't clear to the young men how things would turn out, but one thing *was* clear: they knew who they were in God and that was enough.

We're finally at the top of the mountain, my friend. It's been a long, arduous journey. We've waded through many questions and a lot of tension. We've tried to grapple with ourselves and wrestle with God. Consider reaching this point as a victory for yourself. If even one thing penetrated your heart or caused you to think deeply about your own life and the lives of others, you've achieved something.

The summit of this conversation isn't a destination, nor is it a place to live. Just like any high mountaintop, there is no life there; there is only perspective. Take in the view. Capture the clarity of the moment. Use these thoughts and memories as a map for your journey back down into the valley of life, where true fruit can grow in your life and intimate relationships can be forged with others.

The first part of our journey was looking at the lay of the land. We had to assess what it would take to rise to the top and see things clearly for the first time—to acknowledge the tension and the questions that arise in a mixed life, beginning with, "Where do I fit in?" I hope you've considered your unique upbringing and identified moments when you were forced to choose sides, or when you couldn't identify with either option clearly.

We then dove headfirst into understanding identity from the intent of the Creator. Our true ID is the *imago Dei*. I hope you've found that, although things aren't that simple, you can embrace your complexity because God has a unique destiny for you, one that will use all you are and leave nothing wasted. Our identities are not in our identifiers but in the interwoven nature God has designed in us.

When we're faced with issues of how our culture affects our ID, we've learned to take a moment to remember that we are not of this earth, just as our King, a King without borders, was not of this earth. We can find power and direction in choosing to follow Jesus and forsaking those leaders of culture who are blind to what really matters and what our hearts are truly searching for—wholeness.

Then we asked, "How do I limit myself?" We dug past all the forms and versions of the selves we built out of a desperation to be accepted. Maybe you've discovered how you tend to morph from situation to situation and identified lids you've put on yourself. And hopefully you've discovered there's a better voice to listen to than the critical voice in your own head: Jesus.

He has taken this journey before. He's been there, done that. Our confidence can grow seeing that Jesus was mixed too! He experienced the nuances of life in all the ways you and I do. Being close to him on this journey will yield the greatest lessons as we walk through this ever-changing landscape.

I hope you were as relieved as I was to see how Jesus taught us some footwork. He flawlessly evaded the traps set out by the Enemy, who was looking to dissolve his identity, and handled temptations in a counterintuitive way. And so Jesus teaches us a new way to be human. He not only redeems the broken patterns of our failed example in Adam but also charts a new course in life to take.

Then we saw the rubber meet the road in the life of Paul, who showed us Jesus' faith in real time. We see in him how a complicated backstory can become our greatest superpower. Nothing is wasted, and Jesus is looking to redeem every part of us—all the weaknesses and broken places—and make them strengths.

And why? To help others—not just ourselves. We can take our own identity on a mission. We find empowerment with works and faith working hand in hand, knowing that "all we have is all we need." As God showed us with Moses' story, God knows our names and he calls us by them. He knows our true identity, and he calls it out of us.

On the summit of another mountain, Peter, James, and John once shared a phenomenal moment with Jesus. The story is called the Mount of Transfiguration and can be found in Matthew 17. Jesus was shown in all his glory, alongside Elijah and our friend Moses. If this were a sitcom, the live studio audience would be going bananas. First, two special guest appearances by Moses and Elijah and then God himself! In his excitement, Peter shouted, "Lord, it is good for us to be here. If you wish, I will put up three shelters—one for you, one for Moses and one for Elijah" (v. 4). God interrupted Peter mid-sentence to say, "This is my Son, whom I love; with him I am well pleased. Listen to him!" (v. 5).

Perhaps Peter had a point in trying to make houses for them to stay in on the summit. The shelters he was talking about building weren't tents intended for a short stay but instead permanent residences. Well, my friends, that is not what Jesus had in mind for his followers or for the mountain.

He promptly headed down the mountain, taking the disciples with him.

It feels like this is where we are now, in our *Mixed* conversation. It's time to release it into the world.

Jesus encountered a situation at the foot of the mountain where a boy was manifesting a demon spirit, and the father of the boy was crying out to Jesus, telling him that his disciples could not cast out the spirit. Jesus did so with ease. For the disciples the question became, "Why couldn't we drive it out?" (Matthew 17:19). Jesus' reply was simple. "Because you have so little faith" (v. 20).

Jesus went straight back to work, dealing with the bumps, the failures, the needs, and the real, messy lives around him. The mountaintop had been a place of vision, but down below, life was waiting.

This book wasn't forged for the mountaintop moment alone. It was meant for the faith needed for life in the valleys. And these tools we've been given are not tools to keep for ourselves. Just as Jesus has been generous with his example, along with all men and women in Scripture and throughout church history, so should you be in your daily living. What happens on the mountain can't stay on the mountain. Someone else is looking to start their journey. To see Jesus for the first time. And then to follow him to a place where they can see themselves clearly for the first time too.

The beautiful thing about coming off the mountain is that you come right back into community. There is no greater place to grow in understanding identity than in godly relationship with others, where humility, trust, and vulnerability lie. Where Jesus operates through people to refine the rough edges of our lives, while sending us on missions to be used by him to see hope restored and lives made whole. All of this points to a journey together.

So don't be afraid of complicated conversations in this mixed-up world. It's beautiful and powerful to be mixed. And you were made for it.

ACKNOWLEDGMENTS

Truthfully, this book would not be possible without the support of so many people in my life.

I'd like to thank my publisher Damon Reiss for giving me the honor of writing a book based on my story and the message God has placed on my heart. You took a chance on me, and our conversation after you heard me present this topic for the first time is one I will never forget.

To my editors, Carrie Marrs and Jenn McNeil: This book was a partnership that both of you helped take across the finish line. I could not have been partnered up with a better team that understood the seriousness of the content and helped to carve it into the form it is today. I am blown away by your skill and work ethic to take these complex ideas and bring clarity so that people can hear the message you both have carried with me these past months.

This opportunity opened the floodgates of memories of how many people helped me along the way in my life, shaping the way I understand culture and directing me on how to have a God-shaped worldview.

To my parents, who always kept God at the center of our household: You took on the responsibilities of being in full-time ministry while simultaneously raising me and my sisters well. I owe how strong I am in the faith and where I am in life to you.

To the friends and family members who have discussed these hard topics with me over the years: the conclusions I have drawn and woven into this book would not exist without the long, deep conversations with you, the trusted people God has placed in my life.

To the institutions where I have studied—Oral Roberts University, Lee University, and Southeastern University: Learning to remain a learner has been the greatest takeaway from my studies. The tools I've been given to seek truth effectively have aided in my journey of writing this book.

To Rev. Samuel Rodriguez, whom I owe a lot of these opportunities to: Your leadership and guidance through various seasons have led to some of the greatest life-altering moments in my adult life. Staying grounded in the Word and a love for the Lord has been the example you have shown throughout my time following your lead in public ministry.

Creating this book was a long road through a tough season of multiple life transitions for my wife, Alexis, and me. However, Alexis should take the prime acknowledgment for the rock she has been for me in this journey—through the sickness of our son, the crazy travel schedules, my master's program, my job change, and our relocation across the country. The journey has been more than difficult for her, but she was my champion in this message, and I have a boatload of gratitude for who she has been. This book never would have been finished if it wasn't for her strength and support.

This book is a high-water mark of my life thus far. I have faith that more opportunities will arise for me to share what God would have me share, but I hold all these ideas and revelations with an open hand because it was with the open hand of an available life that God deposited all that I have had to share. There is nothing original about any of these ideas. They are my meager attempts to present, as best as I can, a clarity about following the Lord as he leads us to be who he has created us to be. My prayer is that the Holy Spirit has spoken through these pages as he often does through his servants.

NOTES

Chapter 1: I'm Confused

1. Daniel A. Rodriguez, *A Future for the Latino Church: Models for Multilingual, Multigenerational Hispanic Congregations* (Westmont, IL: IVP Academic, 2011), 37.
2. Barna Group and the Racial Justice and Unity Center, *Beyond Diversity: What the Future of Racial Justice Will Require of U.S. Churches* (Ventura, CA: Barna Group, 2021), 23.
3. Rodriguez, *A Future for the Latino Church*, 21.
4. Max Fisher, "A Revealing Map of the World's Most and Least Ethnically Diverse Countries," *Washington Post*, May 16, 2013, https://www.washingtonpost.com/news/worldviews/wp/2013/05/16/a-revealing-map-of-the-worlds-most-and-least-ethnically-diverse-countries/.
5. Jayoti Das and Cassandra E. DiRienzo, "Is Ethnic Diversity Good for the Environment? A Cross-Country Analysis," *Journal of Environment & Development* 19, no. 1 (March 2010): 91–113, https://www.jstor.org/stable/26199349.

6. Eli Bonilla Jr. (@elibonillajr), "'Homeless' (thoughts of a mixed kid, written in Notes outside a Wingstop)," Instagram photo, July 12, 2020, https://www.instagram.com/p/CCjmZdHninz/.

Chapter 2: Show Me Your ID

1. "Color Blessed with Dr. Derwin Gray," *Jeremiah Johnston Show Podcast*, September 14, 2019, https://christianthinkers.com/2019/09/color-blessed-with-dr-derwin-gray/.
2. Princeton University, "Snap Judgments Decide A Face's Character, Psychologist Finds," *ScienceDaily*, August 23, 2006, https://www.sciencedaily.com/releases/2006/08/060822170919.htm.

Chapter 3: Visitor's Pass

1. Alina Bradford, "Roma Culture: Customs, Traditions & Beliefs," Live Science, November 26, 2018, https://www.livescience.com/64171-roma-culture.html.
2. Ian Hancock, "Romanies and the Holocaust: A Re-evaluation and Overview," in *The Historiography of the Holocaust*, ed. Dan Stone (London: Palgrave Macmillan, 2004), 383–96.
3. Joseph Bever, *The Christian Songster: A Collection of Hymns and Spiritual Songs, Usually Sung at Camp, Prayer, and Social Meetings, and Revivals of Religion; Designed for All Denominations* (Dayton, OH: Printing Establishment of the United Brethren in Christ, 1858).
4. D. A. Carson, *The Expositor's Bible Commentary, Revised Edition: Matthew* (Grand Rapids, MI: Zondervan Academic, 2017).
5. *Merriam-Webster*, s.v. "racism (*n.*)," accessed November 7, 2022, https://www.merriam-webster.com/dictionary/racism.
6. William H. Frey, "The US Will Become 'Minority White' in 2045, Census Projects," Brookings, March 14, 2018, https://www.brookings.edu/blog/the-avenue/2018/03/14/the-us-will-become-minority-white-in-2045-census-projects/.

7. Jacob Couch, "Pastor Sam Rodriguez Encourages Liberty Students to Be Children of Light," Liberty University, September 8, 2021, https://www.liberty.edu/news/2021/09/08/pastor-sam-rodriguez-encourages-liberty-students-to-be-children-of-light/.
8. Alexis Qumsieh Bonilla and Eli Bonilla, "The Israeli-Palestinian Conflict," May, 26, 2021, in The Future is Here, podcast, www.https://www.youtube.com/watch?v=kciyKdObMl0.
Alexis Qumsieh Bonilla and Eli Bonilla, "Palestinian Christians: The Forgotten Minority," in Homies and Heroes, May 18, 2021, podcast, https://www.youtube.com/watch?v=gEMANuzgCf8.
Alexis Qumsieh and Amanda Stockton, "Lee University Chapel Series," filmed with Jimmy Harper, March 21, 2017, YouTube video, https://www.youtube.com/watch?v=-8cQF_LCvqI.

Chapter 4: Breaking Out of the Box

1. Jordan Mark Sandvig, "Is America Really a Third World Country in a Gucci Belt?" *The High Low* (blog), August 11, 2020, https://highlowblog.com/is-america-really-a-third-world-country-in-a-gucci-belt/.
2. Jack Ashcraft, "Is the Road to Hell Really Paved with Good Intentions?" Christianity.com, September 1, 2021, https://www.christianity.com/wiki/heaven-and-hell/what-does-the-road-to-hell-is-paved-with-good-intentions-mean.html.
3. Steve Corbett and Brian Fikkert, *When Helping Hurts: How to Alleviate Poverty without Hurting the Poor . . . and Yourself* (Chicago: Moody, 2014), 61–62, 64.
4. Nadia Bolz-Weber, *Accidental Saints: Finding God in All the Wrong People* (Colorado Springs: Convergent Books, 2015), 47.
5. Gordon Heltzel and Kristin Laurin, "Polarization in America: Two Possible Futures," *Current Opinion in Behavioral Sciences*

34 (August 2020): 179–84, https://doi.org/10.1016/j.cobeha
.2020.03.008.

6. *Merriam-Webster*, s.v. "politics (*n.*)," accessed November 7,
2022, https://www.merriam-webster.com/dictionary/politics.

Chapter 5: Building Your Own Box

1. Jonathan Bailey, "Code-Switching and Citation," *Plagiarism
Today*, August 2, 2018, https://www.plagiarismtoday
.com/2018/08/02/code-switching-and-citation.
2. "The Chameleon Effect: Accents and Assimilation," *Cartus*
(blog), August 29, 2017, https://www.cartus.com/en/blog
/chameleon-effect/.
3. *Black Mirror*, created by Charlie Brooker, IMDb.com, accessed
November 7, 2022, https://www.imdb.com/title/tt2085059/.
4. *The Social Dilemma*, directed by Jeff Orlowski-Yang, written
by Vickie Curtis, Davis Coombe, and Jeff Orlowski-Yang (Los
Angeles: Exposure Labs Production, 2020), https://www
.netflix.com/title/81254224.
5. S. Dixon, "Facebook Monthly Active Users (MAU) in the
United States and Canada As of 3rd Quarter 2022," Statista,
October 2022, https://www.statista.com/statistics/247614
/number-of-monthly-active-facebook-users-worldwide/.
6. Majid Fotuhi, "What Social Media Does to Your Brain,"
NeuroGrow, September 21, 2020, https://neurogrow.com
/what-social-media-does-to-your-brain/; Joseph Firth et al.,
"The 'Online Brain': How the Internet May Be Changing Our
Cognition," *World Psychiatry* 18, no. 2 (May 2019): 119–29,
https://doi.org/10.1002/wps.20617.
7. Derek Lartaud, "Who Gets Imposter Syndrome, and How Do
You Deal with It?" KQED, August 18, 2021, https://www.kqed
.org/education/535277/who-gets-imposter-syndrome-and-how
-do-you-deal-with-it.

NOTES

Chapter 6: Straight Out of Nazareth

1. Charles Bridges, "Charles Bridges on Proverbs 4:23," *Reading the Bible with Dead Guys* (blog), Crossway, February 16, 2015, https://www.crossway.org/articles/reading-the-bible-with -dead-guys-charles-bridges-on-proverbs-423/.
2. Robert Chao Romero, *Brown Church: Five Centuries of Latina/o Social Justice, Theology, and Identity* (Westmont, IL: IVP Academic, 2020), 32.
3. Sabine R. Huebner, *Papyri and the Social World of the New Testament* (Cambridge: Cambridge University Press, 2019), 66.

Chapter 7: A New Way to Be Human

1. Jonathan T. Pennington, *The Sermon on the Mount and Human Flourishing: A Theological Commentary* (Grand Rapids, MI: Baker Academic, 2018), 5.

Chapter 8: Of Jews and Gentiles

1. Mike Berardino, "Mike Tyson Explains One of His Most Famous Quotes," *South Florida Sun Sentinel*, November 9, 2012, https://www.sun-sentinel.com/sports/fl-xpm-2012-11 -09-sfl-mike-tyson-explains-one-of-his-most-famous-quotes -20121109-story.html.
2. "No Plan Survives First Contact with the Enemy," Quote Investigator, May 4, 2021, https://quoteinvestigator.com/2021 /05/04/no-plan/.
3. Robert E. Picirilli, *Paul the Apostle: Missionary, Martyr, Theologian* (Chicago: Moody, 1986), 14–15.
4. Steve Jobs, Commencement Speech at Stanford University, June 12, 2005, https://news.stanford.edu/2005/06/12/youve -got-find-love-jobs-says/.

From the Publisher

GREAT BOOKS

ARE EVEN BETTER WHEN THEY'RE SHARED!

Help other readers find this one:

- Post a review at your favorite online bookseller

- Post a picture on a social media account and share why you enjoyed it

- Send a note to a friend who would also love it—or better yet, give them a copy

Thanks for reading!

ABOUT THE AUTHOR

Eli Bonilla Jr. is the father to two beautiful children, Novalee Grace and Ezekiel Eliezer Rafat, and husband to Alexis Gabriella Bonilla. As an emerging leader in the NextGen space, he serves several national networks in various roles, including the NextGen regional cochair for North America with Empowered21 and the national millennial director for the National Hispanic Christian Leadership Conference (NHCLC).